ENTREPRENEURSHIP ECONOMICS

COUNCIL FOR
**Economic
Education**

Teaching Opportunity®

AUTHORS:

Barbara Flowers
Senior Economic Education Specialist
Federal Reserve Bank of St. Louis*

Brent D. Hales
Professor of Economic and Workforce Development
University of Southern Mississippi

Gregory Valentine
Professor of Business Education
University of Southern Indiana

CONTENT ADVISOR:

John Clow
Director of Business Education Programs, Retired
State University of New York at Oneonta

PROJECT COORDINATORS:

Christopher Caltabiano
Vice President, Program Administration
Council for Economic Education

Nichola Tucker
Senior Associate, Program Administration
Council for Economic Education

DESIGN & EDITORIAL:

CCI

This publication was made possible through the generous support of The UPS Foundation.

ISBN: 978-1-56183-735-9

*Views expressed in this volume are those of the authors and do not necessarily represent those of the Federal Reserve Bank of St. Louis or the Federal Reserve System.

CONTENTS

ABOUT THIS VOLUME

It is often said that today's education curriculum is rooted in yesterday's economy, and that a changing, entrepreneurial and technologically driven economy requires different educational approaches. The skill set needed to succeed in the 21st century workforce—one that values opportunity, creativity and agility—is quite different from the skill set needed during the last century. The key to success is an economic way of thinking, which should be a cornerstone of the nation's efforts to reform the educational system.

The nation's economy will increasingly rely on entrepreneurs to stimulate economic growth—and yet even though a growing majority of the nation's students would like to start and own a business, most are ill-prepared to do so. As educators, we can and should provide students with this critical knowledge. And even though not all students who receive entrepreneurship education intend to pursue a career path as an entrepreneur, everyone can benefit from the learning associated with understanding the concepts and processes of economics and entrepreneurship.

Effective entrepreneurship education assists students in achieving economic autonomy and empowerment. With this publication, *Entrepreneurship Economics,* CEE aims to provide high school educators with lessons that place entrepreneurship within this broader economic context.

Entrepreneurship Economics contains 11 lessons featuring student-centered instructional methods and providing teachers with the conceptual frameworks they need to cover entrepreneurship and economics topics in an engaging way. Each of these lessons is designed to stand alone, although they are, of course, closely related to each other.

Lesson 1 introduces students to entrepreneurship through a resource market simulation, which demonstrates how entrepreneurship promotes economic activity and benefits society. Lesson 2 explores economic systems and asks students to analyze the entrepreneur's role in the economy. Lesson 3 personalizes the supply chain by asking students to explore the role regional resources and assets play in local business development and to identify entrepreneurial opportunities within their community. Lesson 4 reviews forms of business ownership and asks students to use this knowledge to make decisions for several entrepreneurial scenarios. Lesson 5 outlines the explicit and implicit costs of entrepreneurship and encourages students to assess the value of their labor in an entrepreneurial venture. Lesson 6 introduces the concepts of risk and insurance and looks at how entrepreneurs can manage risk. Lesson 7 uses a family lending case study and several start-up scenarios to familiarize students with the financing options available to entrepreneurs throughout the various stages of their businesses. Lesson 8 emphasizes the importance of personal financial management to the entrepreneur and explores how the entrepreneur's credit rating affects his or her ability to secure start-up financing. Lesson 9 reviews the concept of human capital within the context of entrepreneurship and encourages students to reflect on their own human capital and entrepreneurial qualities. Lesson 10 illustrates the importance of marketing to entrepreneurship and engages students in the development of a marketing strategy for a given product. Lesson 11 serves as the publication's culminating activity; by conducting a gap analysis, creating a business plan, and delivering an elevator pitch, students synthesize and apply the concepts covered in this book.

Many people are responsible for bringing this publication to completion, starting with Richard MacDonald, who identified the need for this project, and Christopher Caltabiano, who recruited the team of entrepreneurship and economics experts needed to develop this project successfully. Lesson authors Barbara Flowers, Brent Hales, and Greg Valentine worked hard to deliver quality classroom lessons, ever willing to review and revise their work to make this publication as engaging and teacher-friendly as possible. Content advisor John Clow gave invaluable feedback on lesson drafts, and his many years of experience in entrepreneurship education greatly benefited this publication. Project coordinator Nichola Tucker provided the direction needed to get this project to the finish line, and her significant contributions to lesson content ensured the quality of this publication.

Finally, CEE gratefully acknowledges The UPS Foundation, whose generous support made this publication possible.

Council for Economic Education

CORRELATION OF LESSONS WITH NATIONAL STANDARDS IN ECONOMICS*

	L 1	L 2	L 3	L 4	L 5	L 6	L 7	L 8	L 9	L 10	L 11
1. Scarcity				•	•		•				
2. Decision Making				•	•	•	•	•	•		
3. Allocation		•									
4. Incentives		•		•		•					
5. Trade											
6. Specialization											
7. Markets and Prices		•								•	
8. Role of Prices										•	
9. Competition and Market Structure	•	•		•						•	
10. Institutions				•							
11. Money and Inflation											
12. Interest Rates							•				
13. Income							•	•	•		
14. Entrepreneurship	•	•	•	•	•	•	•	•	•	•	•
15. Economic Growth											
16. Role of Government and Market Failure											
17. Government Failure											
18. Economic Fluctuations											
19. Unemployment and Inflation											
20. Fiscal and Monetary Policy											

*Standards taken from *Voluntary National Content Standards in Economics, 2nd ed.*, Council for Economic Education, 2010

CORRELATION OF LESSONS WITH NATIONAL STANDARDS IN PERSONAL FINANCE EDUCATION*

	L 1	L 2	L 3	L 4	L 5	L 6	L 7	L 8	L 9	L 10	L 11
Financial Responsibility and Decision Making											
Apply reliable information and systematic decision making to personal financial decisions											
1. Take responsibility for personal financial decisions							•	•			
2. Find and evaluate financial information from a variety of sourcesfinancial information from a variety of sources							•				•
3. Summarize major consumer protection laws											
4. Make financial decisions by systematically considering alternatives and consequences			•				•	•			•
5. Develop communication strategies for discussing financial issues			•				•				•
6. Control personal information											•
Income and Careers											
Use a career plan to develop personal income potential											
1. Explore career options				•	•	•			•		•
2. Identify sources of personal income			•						•		•
3. Describe factors affecting take-home pay											
Planning and Money Management											
Organize personal finances and use a budget to manage cash flow											
1. Develop a plan for spending and saving							•				
2. Develop a system for keeping and using financial records							•				•
3. Describe how to use different payment methods							•				
4. Apply consumer skills to purchase decisions											
5. Consider charitable giving											
6. Develop a personal financial plan							•				
7. Examine the purpose and importance of a will											

*Standards taken from *National Standards in K-12 Personal Finance Education*, Jump$tart Coalition for Personal Financial Literacy, 2007

CORRELATION OF LESSONS WITH NATIONAL STANDARDS IN PERSONAL FINANCE EDUCATION CONT'D

	L 1	L 2	L 3	L 4	L 5	L 6	L 7	L 8	L 9	L 10	L 11
Credit and Debt											
Maintain creditworthiness, borrow at favorable terms, and manage debt											
1. Identify the costs and benefits of various types of credit							●				
2. Explain the purpose of a credit record and identify borrowers' credit report rights							●	●			
3. Describe ways to avoid or correct debt problems							●	●			
4. Summarize major consumer credit laws											
Risk Management and Insurance											
Use appropriate and cost-effective risk management strategies											
1. Identify common types of risks and basic risk management methods						●					●
2. Explain the purpose and importance of property and liability insurance protection						●					
3. Explain the purpose and importance of health, disability, and life insurance protection											
Saving and Investing											
Implement a diversified investment strategy that is compatible with personal goals											
1. Discuss how saving contributes to financial well-being			●								
2. Explain how investing builds wealth and helps meet financial goals			●								
3. Evaluate investment alternatives			●						●		
4. Describe how to buy and sell investments											
5. Explain how taxes affect the rate of return on investments											
6. Investigate how agencies that regulate financial markets protect investors											

ENTREPRENEURSHIP ECONOMICS © COUNCIL FOR ECONOMIC EDUCATION, NEW YORK, NY

CORRELATION OF LESSONS WITH NATIONAL STANDARDS FOR BUSINESS EDUCATION*

	L 1	L 2	L 3	L 4	L 5	L 6	L 7	L 8	L 9	L 10	L 11
Entrepreneurship											
I. Entrepreneurs and Entrepreneurial Opportunities											
A. Characteristics of an Entrepreneur	●	●	●						●		
B. Role of the Entrepreneur in Business	●	●	●		●				●		
C. Opportunity Recognition and Pursuit	●	●	●	●	●		●	●	●		●
D. Problem Identification and Solutions			●				●				
II. Marketing											
A. Identifying the Market										●	●
B. Reaching the Market			●		●					●	●
C. Keeping/Increasing the Market			●							●	●
III. Economics											
A. Economic Concepts			●		●		●		●		●
B. Market Economy Characteristics		●									
C. Function of Price											
D. Role of Profit and Risk					●						
E. Role of Government											
IV. Finance											
A. Determining Cash Needs											●
B. Identifying Sources and Types of Funding							●	●			●
C. Interpreting Financial Statements					●						
V. Accounting											
A. Keeping Business Records							●				
B. Identifying Types of Business Records							●				
C. Establishing and Using Business Records							●				
D. Interpreting Business Records											
VI. Management											
A. Establishing a Vision											●
B. Hiring Employees											
C. Building Teams											
D. Monitoring Achievement											

*Standards taken from *National Standards for Business Education*, National Business Education Association, 2007

CORRELATION OF LESSONS WITH NATIONAL STANDARDS FOR BUSINESS EDUCATION CONT'D

	L 1	L 2	L 3	L 4	L 5	L 6	L 7	L 8	L 9	L 10	L 11
VI. Management - Cont'd											
D. Managing Risks							•				
VII. Global Markets											
A. Cultural Differences											
B. Import/Export Opportunities											
C. Global Trends											
VIII. Legal											
A. Forms of Business Ownership			•	•							•
B. Government Regulations											
C. Business Ethics											
IX. Business Plans											
A. Develop a business plan											•

CORRELATION OF LESSONS WITH NATIONAL STANDARDS FOR ENTREPRENEURSHIP EDUCATION*

	L 1	L 2	L 3	L 4	L 5	L 6	L 7	L 8	L 9	L 10	L 11
Entrepreneurial Skills											
A. Entrepreneurial Processes											
Discovery			●					●	●		●
Concept Development				●		●					●
Resourcing					●		●	●			●
Actualization			●			●					●
Harvesting											●
B. Entrepreneurial Traits/Behaviors											
Leadership	●	●		●		●		●	●		●
Personal Assessment					●				●		
Personal Management							●		●		●
Ready Skills											
C. Business Foundations											
Business Concepts	●	●	●	●		●	●			●	●
Business Activities			●			●		●		●	●
D. Communications and Interpersonal Skills											
Fundamentals of Communication									●		
Staff Communications											
Ethics in Communication											
Group Working Relationships									●		
Dealing with Conflict									●		
E. Digital Skills											
Computer Basics											
Computer Applications											
F. Economics											
Basic Concepts	●	●	●		●		●		●	●	
Cost-Profit Relationships	●						●				
Economic Indicators/Trends											
Economic Systems	●	●	●			●					
International Concepts											

*Standards taken from *National Content Standards for Entrepreneurship Education*, Consortium for Entrepreneurship Education, 2004

CORRELATION OF LESSONS WITH NATIONAL STANDARDS FOR ENTREPRENEURSHIP EDUCATION CONT'D

	L 1	L 2	L 3	L 4	L 5	L 6	L 7	L 8	L 9	L 10	L 11
G. Financial Literacy											
Accounting								•			
Finance											
Money Management								•			
H. Professional Development											
Career Planning									•		
Job-Seeking Skills									•		
Business Functions											
I. Financial Management											
Accounting											
Finance						•		•			
Money Management			•					•			
J. Human Resource Management											
Organizing											
Staffing											•
Training/Development											
Morale/Motivation											
Assessment											
K. Information Management											
Record Keeping							•				•
Technology											
Information Acquisition											
L. Marketing Management											
Product/Service Creation			•				•			•	•
Marketing-information Management										•	•
Promotion										•	•
Pricing											•
Selling											•

CORRELATION OF LESSONS WITH NATIONAL STANDARDS FOR ENTREPRENEURSHIP EDUCATION CONT'D

	L 1	L 2	L 3	L 4	L 5	L 6	L 7	L 8	L 9	L 10	L 11
M. Operations Management											
Business Systems			●								
Channel Management			●								
Purchasing/Procurement											
Daily Operations											
N. Risk Management											
Business Risks						●					
Legal Considerations				●		●					
O. Strategic Management											
Planning			●								●
Controlling											●

DOWNLOADING VISUALS, ACTIVITIES, AND RELATED MATERIALS

On the Web

To download the visuals and activities for each lesson, find online lessons to extend the student activities, and find related materials to each lesson, visit:

www.councilforeconed.org/entrep-econ

Lesson 1

Entrepreneurship's Many Beneficiaries

Lesson 1
Entrepreneurship's Many Beneficiaries

LESSON DESCRIPTION

This lesson introduces students to **entrepreneurship** and asks them to consider the benefits of entrepreneurial activity. Students will investigate how entrepreneurs benefit those who supply resources. By simulating a resource market, with an increasing number of businesses demanding a fixed amount of resources, students will trace the positive effect on suppliers' revenues. Finally, students will examine the benefits to workers by comparing the number of jobs created by small and large businesses.

INTRODUCTION

Entrepreneurial behavior promotes economic activity that benefits all of us. Entrepreneurial activity serves the **entrepreneur** by providing him or her the freedom to pursue personal business interests, the chance to achieve recognition, the satisfaction of creating new products or improving existing ones, and the opportunity to earn a profit. For consumers, entrepreneurial activity promotes better quality goods and services, better customer service, and lower prices. Those who provide resources to the entrepreneur see their sales and revenues increase. Workers benefit because approximately one-half of all jobs are created by small business. This employment provides wages with which employees support families.

CONCEPTS

- Entrepreneur
- Entrepreneurship
- Revenue
- Surplus
- Shortage

OBJECTIVES

Students will:

1. State the benefits of entrepreneurial behavior to entrepreneurs, consumers, suppliers, workers, and society as a whole.

2. List traits of entrepreneurs.

3. Define **revenue.**

4. Explain changes in prices as a result of **shortages** and **surpluses.**

5. Explain the role of small business in job creation.

TIME REQUIRED

Two class periods

MATERIALS

- Activity 1: The Benefits of Entrepreneurship

- Activity 2: Are Small Businesses the Biggest Producers of Jobs?

- Visual 1: The Benefits of Entrepreneurship

- Visual 2: From Rags to Riches

- Visual 3: Small Businesses – Big Employers

PROCEDURE

1. Explain to students that, in this lesson, they will see how entrepreneurial activity benefits other actors in the economy. Display Visual 1: The Benefits of Entrepreneurship. Work through the different actors identified on the visual using the following steps.

2. *The entrepreneur.* Explain that the entrepreneur benefits from entrepreneurial activity in a number of ways. Ask students for their ideas of how entrepreneurs benefit. Be sure that they understand four benefits in particular: First, the entrepreneur has the freedom to pursue personal business interests rather than following the directives of someone else. Second, he or she has a chance to achieve recognition. Third, the entrepreneur receives the satisfaction of creating new products or improving existing ones. Finally, he or she is entitled to all profit earned by the firm he or she creates.

3. *Those who purchase the entrepreneur's product.* Explain that consumers benefit from entrepreneurial activity because the competition among entrepreneurs promotes better quality goods and services, better customer service, and lower prices.

4. *Those who provide resources to the entrepreneur.* Explain to students that they are going to take part in a short demonstration that will help them understand how resource suppliers benefit from entrepreneurial activity. Write the word "Revenue" on the board. Define revenue as the income businesses receive from the sale of a resource, good or service. From Activity 1: The Benefits of Entrepreneurship, cut out and distribute the eight Wood Wholesaler cards and four New Business cards, one card per student, to twelve students. Explain to the entrepreneurs with new businesses that their goal is to purchase one unit of wood. Instruct students that they should try to spend no more than $50 for the unit of wood, but may need to be flexible in their purchase price based on market conditions. Tell the wood wholesalers that their goal is to sell their unit of wood. Instruct students that should try to sell their unit of wood for no less than $50, but may need to be flexible in the sale price based on market conditions. Point out to both entrepreneurs and wood wholesalers

that the first offer may not be the best offer, and they should shop around before completing their transaction. Instruct each wood wholesaler to write the amount he or she received for the unit of wood on the board under "Revenue." Tell students not to trade cards. When each entrepreneur has one unit of wood, ask all students to take their seats and total the transactions on the board.

5. Allow the first "Revenue" column to remain visible and begin a second "Revenue" column on the board. Distribute four more New Business cards to four additional students. Review the rules, as laid out in Procedure 4. Instruct each wholesaler to write the amount he or she received for the unit of wood on the board in the second "Revenue" column. When each entrepreneur has a unit of wood, ask all students to take their seats and total the transactions. Note that total revenues have increased due to more suppliers having an opportunity to sell wood. However, the increase in revenues may also be due to an increase in the price of wood. If this is the case, ask students to explain the increase in the price *(More entrepreneurs were demanding wood, which brought about an increase in price).*

6. Add a third "Revenue" column on the board. Distribute four more New Business cards to four additional students. Review the rules, as laid out in Procedure 4. Instruct the wood wholesaler to write the amount he or she received for the unit of wood on the board in the third "Revenue" column. When all of the wood is sold, have students take their seats. Ask the following questions.

A. In the first round, how much did the new businesses have to pay for a unit of wood?

Answers will vary, but each should have paid less than $50.

B. Why were the new businesses able to get wood for less than $50?

There was a surplus of wood, meaning that there were more wood wholesalers selling wood than there were new businesses buying wood.

C. Did each new business receive one unit of wood?

Yes

D. In the second round, what happened to total revenues?

They increased.

E. How much did the new businesses have to pay for a unit of wood?

Answers will vary, but each should have paid $50 or, at least, more than they paid in the first round.

F. Why did new businesses have to pay more for wood in this round?

There were more new businesses demanding wood, but the quantity of wood did not increase.

G. Did each new business receive one unit of wood?

Yes.

H. In the third round, what happened to total revenues for the wood wholesalers?

They increased.

I. How much did the new businesses have to pay for a unit of wood?

Answers will vary, but at least some of them will have paid more than $50.

J. Why did new businesses have to pay more for wood in this round?

There was a shortage of wood, meaning that there were more new businesses, each wanting one unit of wood, than there were wood wholesalers, each selling one unit of wood.

K. How do those who provide resources to businesses benefit from entrepreneurial activity?

Sales and revenues increase.

7. Return to Visual 1 and tell students that you will now discuss the next beneficiary on the list: *Those who are employed by the entrepreneur.* Display Visual 2: From Rags to Riches, and read each short biography. Ask students to suggest adjectives that describe the common traits existing among these individuals *(high energy, initiative, perseverance)*. Explain that among the common traits is the entrepreneurial spirit.

8. Provide students with the following names, and ask them to match the entrepreneur with the biography: Sam Walton, Warren Buffett, William Durant, Amadeo Giannini, Henry Ford. Provide the names of these entrepreneurs' companies if students are uncertain.

    a. *Sam Walton – Walmart*

    b. *Warren Buffett – Berkshire Hathaway*

    c. *William Durant – General Motors*

    d. *Amadeo Giannini – Bank of America*

    e. *Henry Ford – Ford Motor Company*

9. Explain that these five companies are among the *Forbes* list of top ten companies (by revenue) in 2011. Point out that even the largest American companies began with an entrepreneur's idea and drive.

10. Ask students to name some small businesses in their neighborhoods. Ask how many people might be employed by each entrepreneur and record student answers on the board.

11. Explain that supporters of government programs to assist small business often state that small businesses are responsible for the majority of employment in the U.S. Certainly, if you consider employment due to entrepreneurial activity, it would amount to virtually 100 percent of private sector employment. Consider the number of past and present employees at Ford, Bank of America, General Motors, Walmart, and Berkshire Hathaway companies. These five entrepreneurs are responsible for employing millions of workers.

12. Display Visual 3: Small Businesses – Big Employers, and familiarize students with each statistic. You may want to provide a copy for each student.

13. Provide students with a copy of Activity 2: Are Small Businesses the Biggest Producers of Jobs? and instruct students to read the article. When students have finished reading, be sure that students understand the difference between gross and net job gains. Gross job gains refers to the total number of jobs created, without taking into consideration any job losses. Net job gains refers to the number of jobs created after subtracting job losses from total job gains. Then ask students to answer the questions in Part 1 of the activity.

   a. What is a common claim regarding job creation sponsored by small businesses?

   It is commonly claimed that more jobs are created by small businesses than by large businesses.

   b. Does this claim appear to be true?

   Answers will vary. Some students will note that the answer depends on how job creation is measured. When measuring job creation through gross job gains, small businesses appear to create the highest number of jobs. When measuring job creation through net job gains, small businesses do not appear to create as many jobs as is commonly claimed. Accept reasonable responses.

   c. What is the maximum number of employees a business can have and still be considered a small business?

   According to the Small Business Administration, a business is small if it employs fewer than 500 people.

   d. What is being measured by the Gross and Net Job Gains by Firm Size table?

   Average job gains (in thousands) per quarter, from the third quarter of 1992 to the first quarter of 2010

14. Explain that the 2007-2009 recession created an unusually high level of unemployment, so the authors of this study have provided gross and net job gains for the total sample period and for the total sample period, excluding the recession.

15. Tell students that they will analyze the data table more closely to evaluate the claim that small businesses produce the most jobs. Students should focus their analysis on the sample period that excludes the 2007-2009 Recession. Direct students to Part 2 of the activity, which asks them to look at the Size data points in the Gross Job Gains column.

   a. Which size firms created the largest number of jobs?

   1-19 employees

   b. Which size firms created the second-largest number of jobs?

   20 to 99 employees

   c. Does this support or refute claims that small businesses create the largest number of U.S. jobs?

   Support

16. Direct students to Part 3 of the activity, which asks them to look at the Percent of Total data points in the Gross Job Gains column.

   a. On average, what percentage of jobs was created by small businesses with fewer than 20 employees per quarter?

   29.3 percent

   b. On average, what percentage of jobs was created by small businesses with 20 to 99 employees per quarter?

   26.8 percent

   c. On average, what percentage of jobs was created by large firms of 500 or more employees per quarter?

   26.1 percent

d. Do these statistics support or refute the claim that small businesses create the most jobs in the U.S.?

Support

17. Direct students to Part 4 of the activity, which asks them to look at the Size data points in the Net Job Gains column.

a. Which size firms created the largest number of jobs?

500 or more employees

b. Which size firms created the second-largest number of jobs?

20-99 employees

c. Do these statistics support or refute the claim that small businesses create the most jobs in the U.S.?

Refute

d. On average, how many thousands of jobs were created per quarter by firms with fewer than 20 employees?

28,000

e. On average, how many thousands of jobs were created per quarter by firms with 20 to 99 employees?

40,000

f. How does the sum of the jobs created by firms with fewer than 100 employees compare with the number of jobs created by firms with 500 or more employees?

They are equal, at an average of 68,000 per quarter.

g. Does the above comparison support or refute the claim that small businesses create the most jobs in the U.S.?

Refute. The comparison reveals that, when looking at net job gains, small businesses create as many jobs as big businesses.

18. Explain to students that, when measuring job creation through gross job gains, small businesses produce the most jobs. However, the article argues that job creation should be measured through net job gains. This revised approach to measurement at first seems to refute common claims about small business job creation. By analyzing the data more closely, we understand that small businesses with fewer than 100 employees make the same net job gains as large businesses with over 500 employees. While small businesses may not be the biggest producers of jobs, they are absolutely critical to job creation in the U.S.

19. Refer back to the statement on Visual 1, *Those who are employed by the entrepreneur.* Ask students how entrepreneurial activity benefits those who are employed by the entrepreneur. A large number of people, approximately one-half of all employees, are employed by small businesses. This employment provides wages with which employees can support families. Therefore, *society as a whole* benefits.

CLOSURE

Summarize the lesson by discussing the following questions with students:

1. How does entrepreneurial activity benefit the entrepreneur?

Freedom to pursue personal business interests rather than following the directives of someone else; a chance to achieve recognition; the satisfaction of creating new products or improving existing ones; entitlement to all profit earned by enterprise

2. How does entrepreneurial activity benefit those who purchase the entrepreneur's product?

Entrepreneurial activity promotes better quality goods and services, better customer service, and lower prices.

3. How does entrepreneurial activity benefit those who provide resources to the entrepreneur?

Their sales and revenues increase.

4. How does an increase in the number of small businesses affect the demand for resources?

   The demand increases as entrepreneurs increase production.

5. How does a shortage in the market for a resource affect the resource owner's revenue?

   A shortage will increase the price of the resource, and the resource owner's revenue will increase.

6. How does entrepreneurial activity benefit those who are employed by the entrepreneur?

   About one-half of all jobs are created by small business. This employment provides wages with which employees support families.

ASSESSMENT

Constructed-response question

Instruct students to write a brief essay explaining how the entrepreneurial activity of an entrepreneur of the student's choosing benefits/benefited all of society. Students may choose an entrepreneur from history or a present-day entrepreneur. Instruct students to label each section of the essay with the headings from Visual 1.

ACTIVITY 1
THE BENEFITS OF ENTREPRENEURSHIP

Directions: Cut out the following cards and distribute to students. Please note that these cards have been designed for a class of 20 students. If the class is smaller than 20 students, hand out fewer Wood Wholesaler cards.

Wood Wholesaler – one unit of wood	Wood Wholesaler – one unit of wood	Wood Wholesaler – one unit of wood	Wood Wholesaler – one unit of wood
Wood Wholesaler – one unit of wood	Wood Wholesaler – one unit of wood	Wood Wholesaler – one unit of wood	Wood Wholesaler – one unit of wood
New Business – wants one unit of wood	New Business – wants one unit of wood	New Business – wants one unit of wood	New Business – wants one unit of wood
New Business – wants one unit of wood	New Business – wants one unit of wood	New Business – wants one unit of wood	New Business – wants one unit of wood
New Business – wants one unit of wood	New Business – wants one unit of wood	New Business – wants one unit of wood	New Business – wants one unit of wood

Activity 2

Are Small Businesses the Biggest Producers of Jobs?

"Are Small Businesses the Producers of Jobs?" by Kevin L. Kliesen and Julia Maués in *The Regional Economist (April 2011)*

It is often claimed that small firms are responsible for a disproportionately large share of new jobs that are created in the U.S. economy. If true, this speaks well of the entrepreneurial spirit of the U.S. economy, whereby newcomers introduce new ideas or production processes that lead to new and improved products or services. The rise of global companies like Wal-Mart, Microsoft and Google from small beginnings is a testament to the importance of small businesses and the economic forces they sometimes unleash. However, the claim that small businesses generate a large percentage of new jobs must be evaluated carefully. First, there isn't a universal agreement on the definition of a small business. Furthermore, the failure rates of small business are quite high. According to the Bureau of Labor Statistics, only about half of the businesses that opened in 1994 were still operating five years later. Thus, when one accounts for job destruction, small businesses appear to account for a significantly smaller share of net new jobs created in the private sector than many people might believe.

What Do Past Studies Reveal?

The importance of small businesses to job creation has been part of the economic policy narrative for some time. In 1979, then-Massachusetts Institute of Technology Professor David Birch claimed that firms with 20 or fewer employees accounted for two-thirds of all new jobs created between 1969 and 1976; firms with 100 or fewer employees accounted for 82 percent of all new jobs created. Conversely, he found that large firms (500 or more employees) accounted for only 15 percent of net job growth. Birch's finding challenged the conventional wisdom about job creation at the time and, accordingly, had enormous influence on policymakers and researchers.[1]

Some economists soon began to challenge Birch's findings. Using the same data as Birch, Catherine Armington and Marjorie Odle found in 1982 that businesses with 100 or fewer employees accounted for only 39 percent of net new jobs. Several years later, Charles Brown, James Hamilton and James Meddoff pointed out that 40 percent of jobs created in small businesses in 1980 no longer existed in 1986. A more up-to-date assessment of the job-creation characteristic of small businesses can be found in work published by Stephen Davis, John Haltiwanger and Scott Schuh in 1996. These authors noted that "a common confusion between net and gross job creation distorts the overall job creation picture and hides the enormous number of new jobs created by large employers."[2] The authors found that although gross job creation is high for smaller firms (100 or fewer employees), so is job destruction. Slowly, researchers were coming to the conclusion that small businesses did create a lot of new jobs, but the high failure rate of these businesses suggested that their net job creation was much lower.

Gross and Net Job Gains by Firm Size

Earlier this year, a study designed to look at the entire economy was published.[3] The researchers found that small firms create more net jobs than do large firms, which is consistent with the conventional wisdom but generally not the thrust of past research. However, they concede that Birch overestimated the importance of small business in job creation and found that there is a much smaller difference between the net number of new jobs created by large firms and small firms than Birch originally suggested.

Business Employment Dynamics

Researchers who want to assess the claim that small businesses account for a disproportionate percentage of new jobs must

ACTIVITY 2, CONTINUED

ARE SMALL BUSINESSES THE BIGGEST PRODUCERS OF JOBS?

Average job gains (in thousands) per quarter, 1992:Q3 to 2010:Q1				
	Gross Job Gains		Net Job Gains	
Size	Total Sample Period	Excluding 2007-09 Recession	Total Sample Period	Excluding 2007-09 Recession
1 to 19	821	828	16	28
20 to 99	747	758	25	40
100 to 499	496	505	25	37
500 or more	722	739	40	68
TOTAL	2,787	2,831	105	173
Percent of Total				
1 to 19	29.5%	29.3%	15.0%	16.1%
20 to 99	26.8%	26.8%	23.6%	23.1%
100 to 499	17.8%	17.8%	23.4%	21.3%
500 or more	25.9%	26.1%	37.9%	39.4%
TOTAL	100%	100%	100%	100%

Source: Authors' calculations based on Bureau of Labor Statistics' Business Employment Dynamics dataset. Some percentages do not total 100 due to rounding.

first confront several issues. First, what is the best data source for the hypothesis to be tested? Second, how should a small business be defined? (The Small Business Administration says a business is small if it employs fewer than 500 people. However, it may not be wise to lump together a Silicon Valley startup with a relatively large, established manufacturer.) Third, should the focus be on the gross number of jobs created or the net number of jobs created? The research suggests the latter. Why? Because even during the depths of the 2007-09 recession, businesses were still adding an average of nearly 800,000 new jobs a month. But they were shedding an even larger number of jobs per month—about 971,000.

In this article, we use the Business Employment Dynamics (BED) dataset from the Bureau of Labor Statistics.[4] One drawback of the BED is that it has less than 20 years of

history, which may limit the ability to draw firm conclusions. The analysis in this article uses the following breakdown of firm size: 1-19 employees; 20-99 employees; 100-499 employees; and 500 or more employees.

Job Gains by Firm Size

The table shows average gross and net job gains at all private business establishments from the third quarter of 1992 through the first quarter of 2010.[5] Over this roughly 18-year period, gross job gains per quarter averaged a little less than 2.8 million, or about 929,000 per month. Since the 2007-2009 recession was extremely severe, the table includes a separate column that excludes the data from that period. The lower half of the table shows that businesses with fewer than 20 employees provided the largest percentage of gross job gains (about 30 percent). Businesses with

ACTIVITY 2, CONTINUED
ARE SMALL BUSINESSES THE BIGGEST PRODUCERS OF JOBS?

between 20 and 99 employees accounted for the next largest share (about 27 percent), with the largest firms (500 or more) accounting for a somewhat smaller percentage (about 26 percent). The remaining category—businesses with between 100 and 499 employees—accounted for a smaller percentage of gross job gains. All of these percentages are little-changed if we exclude the recession period.

The analysis in the table seems consistent with the conventional wisdom that small businesses are the largest source of job creation in the economy. However, as suggested by previous studies, the conclusion tends to change when the focus switches to net job creation.

The two right-hand columns in the table examine net job gains. Net job gains are defined as job gains minus job losses. Three findings are apparent from the table. First, net job gains were significantly smaller than gross job gains. The net gains per quarter averaged only 105,000, or 35,000 per month. Second, the table shows that the recession dramatically reduced the rate of net job creation. Once net job losses during the recession are removed from the calculation, the number of net jobs rose to 173,000 per quarter (about 58,000 per month). Finally, and perhaps most importantly, the BED data show that since 1992, net job creation tended to be largest among the largest firms: These firms accounted for about 38 percent of the total. The smallest firms showed the smallest percentage of net jobs created. This result does not change if the past recession is excluded from the sample.

In short, small businesses showed higher rates of gross job creation, but they also exhibited high rates of job destruction. Looked at from this standpoint, net job creation matters most.

[1] Birch followed up his original study with several subsequent studies (not cited herein).

[2] One drawback of this study is that it focused on the manufacturing sector, which is a relatively small share of the economy and, thus, probably not a good representation of total job creation.

[3] See Neumark, David; Wall, Brandon; and Zhang, Junfu. "Do Small Businesses Create More Jobs? New Evidence for the United States from the National Establishment Time Series." The Review of Economics and Statistics, February 2011, Vol. 93, No. 1, pp. 16-29

[4] The BED is a quarterly series that is based on the Quarterly Census of Employment and Wages, which uses state unemployment insurance records. See Spletzer et al. for more information about the BED.

[5] Changes in employment can arise from opening or expanding businesses, or closing or contracting businesses. Gross job gains include the sum of all jobs added at both opening and at expanding establishments. Gross job losses, then, include the sum of all jobs lost at both closing establishments or contracting establishments.

REFERENCES

Armington, Catherine; and Odle, Marjorie. "Small Business: How Many Jobs?" *The Brookings Review, Winter 1982*, Vol. 1, No. 2, pp. 14-17.

Birch, David L. *The Job Generation Process.* Cambridge, Mass.: MIT Program on Neighborhood and Regional Change, 1979.

Brown, Charles; Hamilton, James; and Medoff, James. *Employers Large and Small.* Cambridge, Mass.: Harvard University Press, 1990.

Davis, Stephen J.; Haltiwanger, John C.; and Schuh, Scott. *Job Creation and Destruction.* Cambridge, Mass.: MIT Press, 1996.

Haltiwanger, John .C.; Jarmin, Ron C.; and Miranda, Javier. *"Who Creates Jobs? Small vs. Large vs. Young."* NBER Working Paper 16300, August 2010. See www.nber.org/papers/w16300

Neumark, David; Wall, Brandon; and Zhang, Junfu. *"Do Small Businesses Create More Jobs? New Evidence for the United States from the National Establishment Time Series."* The Review of Economics and Statistics, February 2011, Vol. 93, No. 1, pp. 16-29.

Spletzer, James R.; Faberman, R. Jason; Sadeghi, Akbar; Talan, David M.; and Clayton, Richard L. *"Business Employment Dynamics: New Data on Gross Job Gains and Losses."*

Source: http://research.stlouisfed.org/publications/regional/11/04/small_business.pdf

Questions:

Part 1:

a. What is a common claim regarding job creation sponsored by small businesses?

_____

_____

b. Does this claim appear to be true?

_____

_____

c. What is the maximum number of employees a business can have and still be considered a small business?

_____

_____

d. What is being measured by the Gross and Net Job Gains by Firm Size table?

_____

_____

Part 2:

Refer to the Gross Job Gains column, and focus on the Size data points that exclude the 2007-2009 Recession.

a. Which size firms created the largest number of jobs? _____

b. Which size firms created the second largest number of jobs? _____

c. Does this support or refute claims that small businesses create the largest number of U.S. jobs?

_____

Part 3:

Refer to the Gross Job Gains column, and focus on the Percent of Total data points that exclude the 2007-2009 Recession.

a. On average, what percentage of jobs was created by small businesses with fewer than 20

employees per quarter? _____

b. On average, what percentage of jobs was created by small businesses with 20 to 99 employees

per quarter? _____

c. On average, what percentage of jobs was created by large firms of 500 or more employees

per quarter? _____

d. Do these statistics support or refute the claim that small businesses create the most jobs in the U.S.? _____

Part 4:

Refer to the Net Job Gains column, and focus on the Size data points that exclude the 2007-2009 Recession.

a. Which size firms created the largest number of jobs? _____

b. Which size firms created the second-largest number of jobs? _____

c. Do these statistics support or refute the claim that small businesses create the most jobs in the U.S.? _____

d. On average, how many thousands of jobs were created per quarter by firms with fewer than 20 employees? _____

e. On average, how many thousands of jobs were created per quarter by firms with 20 to 99 employees? _____

f. How does the sum of the jobs created by firms with fewer than 100 employees compare with the number of jobs created by firms with 500 or more employees?

_____

_____

g. Does the above comparison support or refute the claim that small businesses create the most jobs in the U.S.? _____

VISUAL 1

THE BENEFITS OF ENTREPRENEURSHIP

Those who benefit from entrepreneurial activity:

1. The entrepreneur

2. Those who purchase the entrepreneur's product

3. Those who provide resources to the entrepreneur

4. Those who are employed by the entrepreneur

5. Society as a whole

Visual 2

From Rags to Riches

a. Born in 1918, he was an Eagle Scout at age 13. He played basketball at his Missouri high school and was quarterback of the state champion football team. He earned a degree in economics at the state public university. He opened a store in Newport, Arkansas and later opened a five and dime in Bentonville.

b. At age 6, he bought six-packs of Coca Cola for $.25 and then sold each bottle for $.05, earning a 5-cent profit on each six-pack. He bought his first stock at age 11, three shares at $38 that he later sold at $40. By age 17, he had earned $5,000 delivering newspapers. He went to college and became a stockbroker in Omaha.

c. He quit high school to work in his grandfather's lumberyard. At age 24, he started a horse-drawn carriage firm, the Flint Road Cart Company. He organized another company in 1908 which was taken by the bank in bankruptcy in 1910. Just one year later, he was able to regain his company.

d. This vegetable seller began a bank in 1904 to help fellow immigrants get their start in the U.S. When the San Francisco earthquake struck, he walked 17 miles to get to his bank. He found it relatively unharmed but with fires raging, he became so concerned, he removed the gold and money from the vault. Disguising it in orange crates, he carted the vault contents to his home. This move kept his bank in business while others had to close due to fire.

e. He grew up on a farm and left home at age 16 to become an apprentice machinist. When he returned home, he worked on steam engines and farm equipment. He began experimenting on internal combustion engines and, after two failed attempts, began a successful company in 1903.

VISUAL 3

SMALL BUSINESSES - BIG EMPLOYERS

- Small businesses employ just over half of U.S. workers. Of 119.9 million nonfarm private sector workers in 2006, small firms with fewer than 500 workers employed 60.2 million and large firms employed 59.7 million. Firms with fewer than 20 employees employed 21.6 million. While small firms create a majority of the net new jobs, their share of employment remains steady since some firms grow into large firms as they create new jobs. Small firms' share of part-time workers (21 percent) is similar to large firms' share (18 percent).

  Source: U.S. Dept. of Commerce, Bureau of the Census: Statistics of U.S. Businesses, Current Population Survey

- Firms with fewer than 500 employees accounted for 64 percent (or 14.5 million) of the 22.5 million net new jobs (gains minus losses) between 1993 and the third quarter of 2008. Continuing firms accounted for 68 percent of net new jobs, and the other 32 percent reflect net new jobs from firm births minus those lost in firm closures (1993 to 2007).

  Source: U.S. Dept. of Labor, Bureau of Labor Statistics, Business Employment Dynamics. Note that the methodology used for the figures above counts job gains or losses in the actual class size where they occurred.

- Seven out of ten new employer firms last at least two years, and about half survive five years. More specifically, according to new Census data, 69 percent of new employer establishments born to new firms in 2000 survived at least two years, and 51 percent survived five or more years. Firms born in 1990 had very similar survival rates. With most firms starting small, 99.8 percent of the new employer establishments were started by small firms. Survival rates were similar across states and major industries.

  Source: U.S Dept. of Commerce, Bureau of the Census, Business Dynamics Statistics. Note that the figures could be skewed slightly by the rare occurrence of new firms opening multiple establishments in their first few years.

THE ROLE OF THE ENTREPRENEUR IN THE ECONOMY

LESSON 2
THE ROLE OF THE ENTREPRENEUR IN THE ECONOMY

LESSON DESCRIPTION

In this lesson, students will explore the purpose of an economic system and differentiate between **market** and **command economies**. Students will review the meaning of **capitalism** and engage with several different critiques of the market economy, exploring the ways in which these criticisms have extended to entrepreneurship. Finally, students will explore counter-arguments to these criticisms and learn how **competition** among entrepreneurs in a free market economy can promote behaviors that increase the welfare of consumers, workers, and society as a whole.

INTRODUCTION

Entrepreneurial activity is the essence of the U.S. economy because the U.S. economy is primarily a capitalist economic system. The term "self-interest," as it applies to capitalism and entrepreneurship, is often interpreted as "greed." Therefore, accusations of unethical behavior and exploitation sometimes obscure the benefits of entrepreneurial activity to consumers and workers. "Greed" and "self-interest" are not synonymous words. In a market-oriented economy, individuals acting in their own self-interest generate economic activity that provides consumers with a larger variety of quality goods and services and workers with a wider choice in employment. Profit-seeking is a critical driver of a market-oriented economy.

CONCEPTS

- Capitalism
- Market economy
- Command economy
- Factors of production
- Competition

OBJECTIVES

Students will:

1. Define and describe capitalism.

2. Differentiate between a market economy and a command economy and explain how resources are allocated differently within the two economic systems.

3. List the four factors of production and provide examples of different types of productive resources.

4. Describe how profit provides incentives and rewards to the entrepreneur.

5. Analyze arguments for and against capitalism and entrepreneurship.

TIME REQUIRED

Two class periods

MATERIALS

- Activity 1: An Interview with Mr. Market and Ms. Command

- Activity 2: Milton Friedman Speaks on Capitalism

- Visual 1: Market vs. Command Economy

- Visual 2: What is Capitalism?

- Visual 3: Factors of Production

- Visual 4: Capitalism Critiques

- Visual 5: The Benefits of Entrepreneurship

- One index card for each student

PROCEDURE

1. Display Visual 1: Market vs. Command Economy, and read aloud the definition of an economic system. Explain to students that an economic system provides a set of rules for how resources are allocated within a group of people or nation.

   Then, read aloud the definition of market economy. Explain that, in a market economy, a business produces goods and/or services with the hope that consumers will purchase them and that the business, in turn, will earn a profit.

   Discuss with students how resources are allocated in a market economic system. Be sure to note the following:

   - In a market economy, consumers influence how resources are used in that the nation's resources are used to make the things that consumers want.

   - The revenue a business generates through selling its goods and services not only pays for the costs of the firm, such as raw materials, labor, and machinery, but also provides entrepreneurs with a profit. Profit incentivizes and rewards the entrepreneur for taking the risk of starting a new business.

   - If consumers are not willing to buy the product or service a business offers, that business will not have the money to buy the resources to continue producing its product, and no profit will be made. If the business continues to fail to generate consumer interest, the firm will go out of business. The business will not continue to use resources to make its goods because the goods are not wanted.

   - On the other hand, if the consumer likes what the business produces and buys the product at a price which covers costs and generates a reasonable profit, resources will continue to be used to make that product.

   Once students have an understanding of a market economy, return to Visual 1 and read the definition of a command economy. Explain that, in a command system, central planners, usually the government, decide what goods and services should be produced and then allocate resources accordingly. Ask students how this is different than in a market economy *(in a market economy, consumers influence how resources are used by creating demand for certain goods and services)*. Emphasize the fact that, in a command economy, the government owns the resources rather than the individuals or groups of individuals in a market economy.

   Tell students that no nation has ever possessed a pure market or command economy. The United States has a market-oriented economy, but the government still controls a portion of its economy. This is why we call the United States' economy a mixed market system. While the market makes most decisions as to how resources are allocated, the government does make some decisions, such as those regarding schools, military, and fire/police protection. Similarly, no economy has ever possessed a completely command economy. Nations such as Cuba, China, and North Korea have economies that are primarily command economies. However, even the strictest command economy allows some market activity, such as allowing individuals to sell some of their produce or handiwork locally.

2. To reinforce these concepts, hand out one copy of Activity 1: An Interview with Mr. Market and Ms. Command to each student. Ask three students to play the roles of interviewer, Mr. Market, and Ms. Command. After the interview is performed, give students time to answer the questions that follow the interview. Review students' answers in a class-wide discussion.

   a. What is an economic system?

      An economic system provides a set of rules for how resources are allocated within a particular country or group of people.

b. What are the four factors of production?

Natural Resources, Labor, Capital Goods, and Entrepreneurship

c. Describe the primary difference between a command economy and a market economy when deciding how resources are to be used?

Individuals, through their decisions in the marketplace, decide what will be produced in a market economy. Central planners, generally in government, make the decisions as to what will be produced and how it is will be produced in a command economy.

d. How is property ownership different in a market economy compared to a command economy?

Individuals own the resources in a market economy whereas the government owns the resources in a command economy.

e. What are the freedoms that individuals have in a market economy that they do not have in a command economy?

Individuals in a market economy have greater freedom of choice. In a market economy, there is more variety in products and work options, and individuals possess the freedom to start their own businesses.

f. What is a market? How does it decide how resources are allocated?

A market is wherever buyers and sellers meet. In a market economy, consumers are free to purchase what they want. If sellers can cover costs and make a profit from the sale of their goods and services, they will be able to purchase resources. Thus, resources are used to make products that are beneficial to both the buyers and sellers.

g. What is the role of government in a market economy and in a command economy?

Government plays a minimal role in a market economy by simply making sure that the markets are competitive. Government plays a major role in a command economy by making most of the decisions about what will be produced, how it will be produced, and who will get the produced items.

h. Why are entrepreneurs more important in a market economy than in a command economy?

In a market economy, entrepreneurs are rewarded with profit if they provide something that the consumer wants, The market economy wants new and better products at a lower price, which entrepreneurs provide. Since individual initiative is not as important in a command economy, the entrepreneur plays a much lesser role in the economy; resource decisions are made by a central committee, not by individual entrepreneurs.

i. Is there any economy in the world that is strictly a market economy or a command economy? Explain your answer.

There are economies which are primarily market economies or command economies. However, each economic system has a sector that possesses characteristics of the other. Market-oriented economies include some central planning, and command economies allocate some resources according to the market.

3. Tell students that capitalism is another name for a market-oriented economy. Ask students to describe their understanding of capitalism. Discuss student responses. Display Visual 2: What is Capitalism? Review the definition of capitalism, and confirm students' understanding of the term by asking them to paraphrase the definition.

4. Display Visual 3: Factors of Production, and reveal the definitions for natural and capital resources. (Note that the concepts

in Visual 3 have already been covered in the interview with Mr. Market and Ms. Command.) Review each factor of production, and explain that, under capitalism, private citizens can own natural and capital resources, meaning that private citizens can determine the use of those resources.

Next, reveal the definition of human resources and explain that ownership of human resources—also known as labor—belongs to the individual providing the labor. Capitalists believe that, as owners of their own labor, they are free to sell their labor to whomever is willing to buy it. The successful sale of labor depends on several factors, the most important of which is the quality of labor, as developed through education and training.

Finally, reveal the definition of entrepreneurship. Explain that entrepreneurship can only exist under capitalism because the entrepreneur must be free to own a business, to acquire the resources necessary, and to earn a profit. If resources are owned by the state under a command system, then entrepreneurs have no access to organizing a business. Even if they are allowed to purchase resources, they are not allowed to retain the profit from a business because businesses are run by the state. In cases where entrepreneurial activity exists, it is because the command system has relaxed to tolerate some level of capitalism.

5. Refer back to the definition of capitalism and explain that a goal of the entrepreneur is to earn a profit. If the entrepreneur is successful in earning a profit, competition will develop as other entrepreneurs take notice and open similar businesses, hoping to generate a profit for themselves. Entrepreneurs that can improve the quality of the product or offer it at a lower price, or both, will win the competition.

6. Explain that competition and the profit motive lead to controversy about capitalism. Write the word "Capitalism" in big letters on the board. Put three columns under the word Capitalism, titled "Supports," "Supports with Some Reservations," and "Rejects." Display Visual 4: Capitalism Critiques, and instruct the students to categorize each quote.

Supports—Warren Buffett

Supports with some Reservations—Winston Churchill, Milton Friedman, Mohandas Gandhi, Abraham Lincoln

Rejects—Karl Marx, Bertrand Russell

Instruct students to re-read the quotes of those who seem to reluctantly support or reject capitalism, and ask for one word that might describe people's criticism of capitalism.

Answers will vary, but students should recognize "greed" as a common theme.

7. Explain that the fairness of alternative economic systems and political systems is a common debate. Distribute Activity 2: Milton Friedman Speaks on Capitalism, and explain to students that Phil Donahue produced and hosted a successful daytime talk show, "The Phil Donahue Show," in the 70s, 80s, and 90s. Milton Friedman was a Nobel Laureate in economics and a highly regarded professor of economics at the University of Chicago.

Ask two students to read the parts of Phil Donahue and Milton Friedman. After the reading, discuss the following questions with the class:

a. What did Donahue mean by the terms "haves" and "have-nots?"

"Haves" are people with access to goods and services; "have-nots" are people without that access.

b. What was Donahue's observation leading to his criticism of capitalism?

There are more "have-nots" than "haves." People with wealth have power in society. People are greedy. People are not rewarded according to their virtue.

c. How does Milton Friedman explain the economic benefits of self-interest?

Friedman explains that when individuals are free to act in their self-interest, their economic benefit also benefits others.

8. Explain to students that criticisms of capitalism are often extended toward entrepreneurs because entrepreneurship embodies the capitalistic spirit. Display Visual 5: The Benefits of Entrepreneurship, and explain that, despite these criticisms, entrepreneurship provides many benefits—to the entrepreneur, to those who purchase the entrepreneur's product, to those who supply resources to the entrepreneur, to those who are employed by the entrepreneur, and to society as a whole. Point out that one criticism of entrepreneurship and capitalism is that profit-seeking leads to "greed" and unethical behavior, particularly cheating customers or exploiting employees. Explain that, with the availability of information, the competition for customers, and the mobility of employees, entrepreneurs who behave unethically risk losing their businesses.

9. Provide an index card to each student. Ask students to think about a small business from which they purchased a good or service in the last month. Instruct them to write the name of the business at the top of the card, followed by a review of that business, focusing on their satisfaction with the service they received, with the good or service they purchased, and with the price they paid.

Collect the cards, and read each one aloud, pausing after each review to allow other students to vote on their likelihood to patronize the business based on the review. Students should vote on a scale of 1 to 5 with "very unlikely" shown as one finger and "very likely" shown as 5 fingers. Assign the student who wrote the review to count the votes and record the name of the company,

the total score, and the average score for that company on the board. (If students have chosen the same business, read each review and allow a vote based on each review.) After each business has been discussed and voted upon, ask the following questions:

a. Did any of the businesses average a 5, indicating that you would be very likely to patronize that business?

Answers will vary.

b. Which businesses appear as the top five?

Answers will vary.

c. What features of these businesses were attractive to you?

Answers will vary, but students will likely suggest that they were impressed with the business's attention to service, the quality of the good or service sold, and/or the price of the good or service.

d. What is the likelihood that these top five businesses remain successful?

Answers will vary, but students should recognize that businesses with good service, quality products, and reasonable prices will remain in business.

e. What businesses appear as the bottom five?

Answers will vary.

f. What features of these businesses shaped your opinion?

Answers will vary, but students will likely comment that reports of poor service, poor quality and/or high prices persuaded them to avoid this business.

g. What is the likelihood that these bottom five businesses remain successful?

Students should recognize that businesses with poor service, shoddy products, and unreasonable prices likely will not remain in business.

Depending on access to the Internet, you may instruct students to conduct searches on several local small businesses. Explain that a site for the business may come up. However, it is also likely that several sites will come up offering consumer reviews of the business. Instruct students to print the reviews and report to the class. Explain that these reviews, along with more organized review services such as Angie's List, Consumer Reports, and the Better Business Bureau allow consumers to report poor service, shoddy quality, and even unethical behavior on the part of small businesses.

10. Explain that a word-of-mouth review process often provides students with information on entrepreneurs as prospective employers. Generally, students work close to home and are likely to know of others who have worked for the local employers. So, students have the ability to learn about an employer and his or her treatment of employees. In addition, labor laws are in place to protect young workers from exploitation. Employers who violate labor laws can be fined or even shut down. At the very least, employers do not want to become known as exploitive because employers compete to attract the best employees.

CLOSURE

Summarize the lesson by discussing the following questions with students:

1. How is capitalism defined?

   Capitalism is an economic system based on private ownership of productive resources and operating businesses in a competitive environment for the purpose of earning a profit.

2. What is a market economy?

   A market economy is one that relies on a system of interdependent market prices to allocate goods, services, and productive resources and to coordinate the diverse plans of consumers and producers, all of them pursuing their own self-interest.

3. What are the characteristics of a market economy?

   Private property, freedom of enterprise and choice, motive of self-interest, competition, system of markets and prices

4. What is a command economy?

   An economy in which most economic issues of production and distribution are resolved through central planning and control

5. What are the characteristics of a command economy?

   Community property, planned economic activity by central committee.

6. What is entrepreneurship?

   A characteristic of people who assume the risk of organizing productive resources to produce goods and services; a resource.

ASSESSMENT
Matching questions

_____ 1. Entrepreneur *(f)*

_____ 2. Market Economy *(a)*

_____ 3. Natural Resources *(e)*

_____ 4. Human Resources *(b)*

_____ 5. Command Economy *(d)*

_____ 6. Capital Goods *(c)*

_____ 7. Capitalism *(g)*

a. An economy based on competition

b. Butcher, baker, candlestick maker

c. Tools and machines

d. An economy employing a central planner in the allocation of resources

e. Gifts of nature used in the production of a good or service.

f. An individual who takes the risk in obtaining resources to produce a good or service.

g. An economic system that promotes private ownership of resource.

Constructed-reponse questions

1. How do entrepreneurs promote economic activity?

   They spearhead the development of new goods and services. If consumers like what they produce, the entrepreneurs add more workers to make the goods or services.

2. What is the role of competition in consumers' access to a variety of goods at acceptable prices?

   Firms compete on the basis of product quality, customer service, and price.

3. What are some criticisms of capitalism?

   It promotes greed and economic inequity.

4. How would Milton Friedman respond to critics of capitalism?

   Answers will vary, but students should explain that when people act in their own self-interest, their efforts benefit others.

5. Why might entrepreneurs who behave unethically risk losing their business?

   Entrepreneurs compete for customers. If they do not offer a quality product at a price acceptable to consumers, consumers will simply turn to a competitor.

ACTIVITY 1
AN INTERVIEW WITH MR. MARKET AND MS. COMMAND

Interviewer: Today, we have with us two people who represent two types of economic systems: Mr. Market Economy and Ms. Command Economy. They are going to tell us about how they are similar and different. Greetings, Mr. Market and Ms. Command. Glad to have you with us today. Now, first thing's first: What exactly is an economic system?

Mr. Market: An economic system is the "rules," so to speak, as to how resources are allocated among a group of people or in a particular country. Now, you may be wondering what I mean by resources. There are four types of resources—also known as **the four factors of production**. There are **natural resources**, which are gifts of nature, such as water, mineral deposits, virgin forests, and land. There are also **capital resources**, which are manmade resources used to produce other items, such as equipment, tools, and buildings. **Labor** is another resource and describes the human effort used to produce goods and services. The final resource is **entrepreneurship**. Entrepreneurs are the people who risk money, time and reputation to organize these resources to produce goods and services. Notice that the last two resources are actually humans— labor as the human effort needed to produce goods and services and the entrepreneur as the individual who organizes the other resources to produce goods and service

Interviewer: Ms. Command, would you agree that an economic system provides rules for how resources are allocated?

Ms. Command: Yes, and this is precisely the area in which we are so different.

Interviewer: What do you mean?

Ms. Command: In my economy, we use central planning to decide how to use resources, what to produce, and what to charge the customer. Generally, it is a central committee, many times the government, who makes decisions about how our natural, capital, labor, and entrepreneurial resources are used. In other words, the central committee decides how many refrigerators get built, what resources should be used to make them, and how the refrigerator will be priced. The central committee even decides who gets refrigerators and who doesn't, because it also decides how much each worker receives in compensation.

Mr. Market: Yes. Your economy, Ms. Command, depends a lot more on group decision-making and group ownership. The central committee makes the decisions, and the government owns the resources. Those are some of the major differences between command and market economies. In my economy, the individual, not the government, owns property. Individuals have the freedom to start their own businesses, and workers have the freedom to decide which jobs they want to pursue with their qualifications. People in a market economy make decisions out of self-interest. If individuals want to start their own businesses because they want to be their own bosses, they can do so. There is a risk in doing that, but many think it is worth the risk because of the potential to make a profit.
Consumers search for goods and services that best satisfy what they want. And workers seek out a job that is the best for them—again satisfying their own self-interest.

ACTIVITY 1, CONTINUED

AN INTERVIEW WITH MR. MARKET AND MS. COMMAND

Interviewer: One thing that always confuses me is the market mechanism, which is an important part of your economic system, Mr. Market. Can you explain that a bit?

Ms. Command: Yes, I want to hear more about what you have to say about the market mechanism.

Mr. Market: A market is where buyers and seller meet. It can be an auction, it can be a store, it can be the Internet—anywhere where buyers and seller get together. Sellers are trying to sell their items at the highest price possible. Buyers are trying to buy at the lowest price possible. There is thus some give and take. If buyers do not want the item that is put on the market or if the item is priced too high, they will not buy it, which means the seller will go out of business because he/she cannot cover costs. Conversely, if a lot of buyers want the product, the business might well expand because the owner would like to make more profit, which is the reward for assuming the risk of starting a business.

Ms. Command: In my system, the committee has to get together to decide what to produce and what not to produce. In your system, it sounds like it is more automatic. That is, if people like and buy the product, more resources are put into making it. If people do not like and buy the product, then resources are not put into making it. The market determines how resources are used instead of a central committee.

Interviewer: I think I understand how a market works a lot better. People in market economies are always talking about competition in a market economy. What role does competition play in your economy?

Mr. Market: Competition plays a very important role. When someone comes up with a new product or service and is making a lot of money, other people see this and want to get in on the action. Multiple people then compete against each other on price, customer service, and product quality. A playing field with a lot of competitors ensures that consumers get a better product at a lower price. Let's take the car industry as an example. Some people buy specific cars which are considered better quality even though they must pay a higher price. Some people buy cars based on price while others buy a particular brand because of a strong local service department.

Ms. Command: In our economy, we do not worry much about competition. We might choose to put out two cars—one that is inexpensive and the other a deluxe car. This means that we'll produce only one inexpensive car and one deluxe car, not multiple versions of each.

Interviewer: How do you ensure, Ms. Command, that the consumer is getting a better product at a lower cost?

Ms. Command: The central committee makes those decisions. Sometimes, this decision-making process takes quite a bit of time. For example, if product deficiencies are discovered, the Central Committee must come to agreement as to what changes must be made.

Interviewer: What is the role of government in both of your economies?

Mr. Market: The role of government is limited when it comes to producing goods and services. The government makes sure that the markets are competitive so that they can operate efficiently.

ACTIVITY 1, CONTINUED

AN INTERVIEW WITH MR. MARKET AND MS. COMMAND

Ms. Command:	Government is generally very important in my economy since it owns the resources and make the decisions as to what to produce, how to produce it, and who is to get the product.
Interviewer:	My last question relates to the entrepreneur. How important is the entrepreneur in each of these economies?
Mr. Market:	The entrepreneur is the individual who drives innovation, making new products that people want. The entrepreneur is the change agent for the economy.
Ms. Command:	Hopefully, the central committee in making the decisions will be entrepreneurial but that cannot always be true. It is many times difficult to get a committee to make a decision which involves taking a risk. Also, there is little incentive for someone to be entrepreneurial because we do not allow individuals for the most part to start their own businesses or make a profit.
Interviewer:	Thank you so much for your comments. This has been very helpful in clarifying the difference between the two economic systems. Oh yes, I forgot to ask. Is there any country in the world which is totally a market or totally a command economy?
Mr. Market:	No, the United States has a mixed economy, tending more toward market than command. This means that many resource decisions are made through the market but others are made through the government. For example, people buy automobiles, homes, and haircuts through the market. Yet, some resource decisions are made by the government, such as those related to national defense, public education, and police/fire protection.
Ms. Command:	I would have to agree with Mr. Market. China, North Korea, and Cuba are examples of countries which are primarily command economies. Yet, they allow some operation of a market, such as for agricultural products. That's why, even in the strictest command economy, you will see fruit and vegetable stands—people raising some products on governmentally owned farms and selling the produce to the general public on a limited scale.

ACTIVITY 1, CONTINUED

AN INTERVIEW WITH MR. MARKET AND MS. COMMAND

Questions

a. What is an economic system?

b. What are the four factors of production?

c. Describe the primary difference between a command economy and a market economy when deciding how resources are to be used.

d. How is property ownership different in a market economy compared to a command economy?

e. What are the freedoms that individuals have in a market economy that they do not have in a command economy?

f. What is a market? How does it decide how resources are allocated?

g. What is the role of government in a market economy and in a command economy?

h. Why are entrepreneurs more important in a market economy than in a command economy?

i. Is there any economy in the world that is strictly a market economy or a command economy? Explain your answer.

ACTIVITY 2

MILTON FRIEDMAN SPEAKS ON CAPITALISM

Phil Donahue: When you see around the globe the mal-distribution of wealth, the desperate plight of millions of people in underdeveloped countries, uh, when you see so few haves and so many have-nots, when you see the greed and the concentration of power, aren't you ever, did you ever have a moment of doubt about capitalism and whether greed's a good idea to run on?

Milton Friedman: Well, first of all, tell me, is there some society you know of that doesn't run on greed? Do you think Russia doesn't run on greed? Do you think China doesn't run on greed? What is greed? Of course, none of us are greedy; it's only the other fellow who's greedy. This, the world runs on individuals pursuing their separate interests. The great achievements of civilization have not come from government bureaus. Einstein didn't construct his theory under order from a, from a bureaucrat. Henry Ford didn't revolutionize the automobile industry that way. The only way the masses have escaped from the kind of grinding poverty you're talking about, the only cases in recorded history were where they have had capitalism and largely free trade. If you want to know where the masses are worse off, worst off, it's exactly in the kinds of societies that depart from that, so that the record of history is absolutely crystal clear, that there is no alternative way, so far discovered, of improving the lot of the ordinary people that can hold a candle to the productive activities that are unleashed by a free enterprise system.

Donahue: But it seems to reward not virtue as much as ability to manipulate the system.

Friedman: And what does reward virtue? Do you think the, uh, communist commissar rewards virtue? Do you think that a Hitler rewards virtue? Do you think, excuse me, if you'll pardon me, do you think American presidents reward virtue? Do they choose their appointees on the basis of the virtue of the people appointed or on the basis of their political clout? Is it really true that political self-interest is nobler somehow than economic self-interest? You know, I think you're taking a lot of things for granted. Just tell me where in the world you find these angels who are going to organize society for us? Well, I don't even trust you to do that. (Laughter.)

Source: http://www.youtube.com/watch?v=76frHHpoNFs

VISUAL 1

MARKET VS. COMMAND ECONOMY

ECONOMIC SYSTEM:
rules about how resources are allocated in a particular country or group of people.

MARKET ECONOMY:

An economy that relies on a system of interdependent market prices to allocate goods, services, and productive resources and to coordinate the diverse plans of consumers and producers, all of them pursuing their own self-interest.

Characteristics of a market economy include:

a. **Private property:** The factors of production are owned by private individuals and private institutions rather than by the government.

b. **Freedom of enterprise and choice:** Entrepreneurs are free to obtain and organize resources to produce and sell goods and services. Consumers are free to purchase goods and services to best satisfy their wants. Workers are free to pursue any job for which they are qualified.

c. **Motive of self-interest:** Entrepreneurs seek profits, consumers seek satisfaction from their use of goods and services, workers seek the highest wages possible.

d. **Competition:** Sellers compete on the basis of price, service and product quality.

e. **System of Markets and Prices:** Markets bring buyers and sellers together and interact with one another with the buyers wanting to get the item at the lowest price and the sellers wanting to sell at the highest price.

f. **Limited Government:** Competitive markets promote the efficient use of resources. Government does not allocate resources, goods or services.

COMMAND ECONOMY:

An economy in which most economic issues of production and distribution are resolved through central planning and control.

Characteristics of a command economy include:

a. **Community property:** There is community ownership of the factors of production – no private ownership.

b. **Planned economic activity:** Production is planned by a central planning unit and resources are assigned as needed

VISUAL 2
WHAT IS CAPITALISM?

Capitalism, a.k.a. private enterprise

An economic system based on the private ownership of the means of production and distribution, characterized by the freedom of capitalists to operate or manage their property for profit in competitive conditions.

VISUAL 3
FACTORS OF PRODUCTION

NATURAL RESOURCES

"Gifts of nature" that can be used to produce goods and services; for example, oceans, air, mineral deposits, virgin forests and actual fields of land.

CAPITAL RESOURCES

Resources and goods made and used to produce other goods and services. Examples include buildings, machinery, tools and equipment.

HUMAN RESOURCES, A.K.A. LABOR

The quantity and quality of human effort available to produce goods and services.

ENTREPRENEURSHIP

The act of being an entrepreneur, one who assumes the risk of organizing productive resources to produce goods and services; a resource.

VISUAL 4
CAPITALISM CRITIQUES

I think the most important factor in getting out of the recession actually is just the regenerative capacity of American capitalism.

Warren Buffett, American business magnate, investor, and philanthropist

The inherent vice of capitalism is the unequal sharing of blessings; the inherent virtue of socialism is the equal sharing of miseries.

Winston Churchill, former prime minister of the United Kingdom

The problem of social organization is how to set up an arrangement under which greed will do the least harm. Capitalism is that kind of a system.

Milton Friedman, American economist

Capital as such is not evil; it is its wrong use that is evil. Capital in some form or other will always be needed.

Mohandas (Mahatma) Gandhi, political and ideological leader of the Indian independence movement

Capital is dead labor, which, vampire-like, lives only by sucking living labor, and lives the more, the more labor it sucks.

Karl Marx, revolutionary socialist and author of The Communist Manifesto

These capitalists generally act harmoniously and in concert, to fleece the people.

Abraham Lincoln, 16th President of the United States

Advocates of capitalism are very apt to appeal to the sacred principles of liberty, which are embodied in one maxim: The fortunate must not be restrained in the exercise of tyranny over the unfortunate.

Bertrand Russell, British philosopher, logician, mathematician, historian, and social critic

VISUAL 5

THE BENEFITS OF ENTREPRENURSHIP

Those who benefit from entrepreneurial activity:

1. The entrepreneur

2. Those who purchase the entrepreneur's product

3. Those who provide resources to the entrepreneur

4. Those who are employed by the entrepreneur

5. Society as a whole

LESSON 3

THE ENTREPRENEUR AND THE SUPPLY CHAIN

LESSON 3
THE ENTREPRENEUR AND THE SUPPLY CHAIN

LESSON DESCRIPTION

This lesson will introduce students to the concept of the **supply chain** by tracing the journey of an "everyday product" from nature to the classroom. By analyzing this "everyday product" and reading a case study about a growing business, students will identify the four main types of businesses that compose the supply chain (manufacturers, wholesalers, retailers, and service providers) and explore the role local **resources** and **assets** play in business development. Finally, students will explore resources and assets in their local community and identify opportunities for entrepreneurs to build businesses using the local supply chain.

INTRODUCTION

For any single product or service, there are many different companies, people, technologies, processes, and resources that move the product or service from supplier to customer. A supply chain is the total system of organizations involved in this move from raw materials to finished product. Effective entrepreneurs understand where their business idea for a new product or service fits into the supply chain. They are able to identify their role as a supplier, manufacturer, wholesaler, retailer, or service provider, and they can develop an efficient, cost-effective system for creating and delivering their product or service. Entrepreneurs must also be able to recognize opportunities to optimize their business's supply chain operations to increase efficiency and reduce costs.

CONCEPTS

- Supply chain
- Assets
- Resources
- Vertical integration

OBJECTIVES

Students will:

1. Understand how and why businesses are created.

2. Define and describe the supply chain.

3. Identify the four types of businesses that compose the supply chain (manufacturers, wholesalers, retailers, and service providers).

4. Explain how different assets impact business development.

5. Examine how regional assets affect the local supply chain and their own business ideas.

TIME REQUIRED

One class period

MATERIALS

- Activity 1: Supply Chain Matching
- Activity 2: Uncle Bill, Inc.
- Activity 3: Building a Business from Assets/Resources
- Visual 1: The Supply Chain
- Visual 2: Asset Analysis

PROCEDURE

1. Hold up an "everyday product," and encourage students to think about the product's origins by asking the following questions. (While you may choose any product that students will be familiar with, the answers below have been modeled on the use of a soda can.)

   a. How did this product get here?

      Possible answers include: purchased from a store or from the school's vending machine; product delivered from a manufacturing plant to the store or vending machine by a truck

b. What goes into making this product?

Possible answers include: water, flavorings, and other chemicals that make up the beverage itself; aluminum and other materials that make up the can; design work that makes up the can's logo and presentation as a product; machine or human labor that gets the beverage into the can

c. What materials make up this product and where do they come from?

- *Water—municipal source*
- *Carbon dioxide to add carbonation—gas plant*
- *Corn for the high fructose corn syrup—farmers*
- *Phosphoric acid—chemical supplier*
- *Kola nuts for caffeine and flavoring—farmers*

d. What are some of the steps that go into making the product?

Answers will vary, but make sure to cover the following steps when discussing students' answers:
- *Formulating the syrup*
- *Manufacturing the syrup*
- *Distributing the syrup to bottlers*
- *Mixing the syrup and carbonated water*
- *Bottling / canning the product*

e. How many companies do you think were involved in getting this product to the classroom?

Answers will vary, but students should understand that many different companies were involved in getting the can of soda to the classroom.

2. Explain to students that the class's discussion of the many different materials and steps that go into making a simple can of soda demonstrates the concept of supply chain. Hand out Visual 1: The Supply Chain. Read aloud and review the definitions provided on the visual with students. Emphasize to students that some businesses focus solely on raw materials while others take already developed products and serve as assemblers of even more complex products. (As you walk students through the visual, you may choose to discuss how the "everyday product" you've chosen for the lesson makes its way through each step of the supply chain.)

3. Hand out Activity 1: Supply Chain Matching. Instruct students to match the appropriate step in the supply chain to the company profiled.

Answers: 1. A; 2. D; 3. B; 4. C; 5. E

4. Explain to students that, as the soda can example shows, the supply chain can involve many different steps and many different companies, each of which contribute to the product based on their area of expertise. In some cases, there are businesses which capture multiple steps of the supply chain. Explain to students that **vertical integration** is a term that describes the degree to which one person or company owns portions of the supply chain. However, remind students that such vertically integrated businesses are not built in a day and are developed over time. Entrepreneurs often start out by analyzing how to use local assets and resources—and by identifying opportunities in the supply chain that they can use to their advantage. Divide students into pairs and hand out Activity 2: Uncle Bill, Inc. Instruct students to read Uncle Bill's story and answer the questions at the end of the activity. Once students are finished, discuss their answers to the questions as a class.

a. What were the businesses that Uncle Bill started?

Fruit and vegetable supply business; nursery; lumber yard; outdoor furniture manufacturer and retailer

b. How did Uncle Bill engage with the supply chain as an entrepreneur?

Uncle Bill recognized opportunities in the assets and resources around him and built businesses throughout the supply chain. Uncle Bill became a manufacturer, wholesaler, and retailer of produce, plants, and furniture.

c. How does Uncle Bill's story demonstrate the concept of vertical integration?

Uncle Bill vertically integrated his businesses by purchasing more of the businesses that supported his other businesses. Over the course of his life, Uncle Bill acquired numerous businesses and captured larger and larger segments of the supply chain.

d. What were the benefits of vertical integration to Uncle Bill's business?

The direct benefits of his investments were many; he didn't have to rely on outside companies to supply products or services to his businesses; he didn't have to pay other companies for raw materials, manufacturing, wholesaling, or retailing, and so he made more profit from his businesses.

e. Although the story focuses on Uncle Bill's success, what might be some of the risks of vertical integration? How might these risks have affected Uncle Bill negatively?

Not every business makes money; some do better than others; by capturing more of the supply chain, Uncle Bill opened himself up to a greater likelihood of failure.

5. Explain to students that Uncle Bill knew that he could grow his businesses in several ways. When he first started out, he used his family's land and the skills that his family taught him to grow his produce. He also used his family's network to sell his produce. He saved his money and acquired more land and thereby developed opportunities to build his

business. The resources that he developed are also known as assets. As he built his businesses, Uncle Bill built up his assets. Over time, he used those assets to acquire more assets. Explain to the students that, like Uncle Bill, effective entrepreneurs know how to recognize and see opportunity in local assets and resources.

6. Distribute one copy of Visual 2: Asset Analysis to students. Discuss with students each of the types of assets. Ask the students the following questions, and discuss their answers as a class:

a. What are some examples of financial assets in our area?

Answers may include banks, credit unions, other lending agencies, existing businesses, economic development agencies, government offices, and civic organizations. Encourage students to get as specific as possible.

b. What are some examples of human assets in our area?

Answers may include schools, colleges, universities, job training programs, existing labor pool such as unemployed workers, existing workers, and students, churches or other faith-based training programs, the military, and other non-traditional programs such as department of corrections programs, and community-based educational and training programs.

c. What are some examples of social assets in our area?

Answers may include social groups, professional organizations, fraternal groups, religious organizations or groups, educational groups, recreational groups, and boards of directors of organizations.

d. What are some examples of cultural assets in our area?

Answers may include local orchestra, historical site or battleground, or sports team.

e. What are some examples of environmental assets in our area?

Answers may include beaches, rivers, lakes, and oceans, parks, national parks, forests, and historic sites, roadways, wildlife, and railways.

f. What are some examples of entrepreneurial assets in our area?

Answers may include chambers of commerce, financial institutions, government-supported services, and business incubators.

7. Divide students into groups of four, and distribute one copy of Activity 3: Building a Business from Assets/Resources to each student. Explain to students that they will work in their groups to identify local assets and develop business ideas based on regional resources. At the conclusion of the activity, call on a representative from each group to describe the group's business idea and explain the business idea's use of local assets. Discuss each group's business idea as a class, identifying the idea's strengths and weaknesses.

CLOSURE

Summarize the lesson by discussing the following questions with students:

1. What is the supply chain?

The supply chain is the total system of organizations and processes that moves a product or service from supplier to consumer. Suppliers, manufacturers, wholesalers, retailers, and service-providers are the main business types that compose the supply chain.

2. Why is the supply chain important to the entrepreneur?

Effective entrepreneurs must understand where their business idea for a new product or service fits into the supply chain. Entrepreneurs must also be able to recognize opportunities to optimize their

business's supply chain operations to increase efficiency and reduce costs.

3. Why is it important for an entrepreneur to investigate the local resources and assets available to him or her?

By exploring the community's resources, the entrepreneur can identify opportunities for new businesses and continued business development.

ASSESSMENT
Multiple-choice questions

1. These assets may be used to train individuals such as schools or job training programs or be the existing labor pool such as unemployed workers, existing workers, and students:

   a. Financial assets
   b. Social assets
   c. Cultural assets
   d. *Human assets**

2. These types of firms take raw materials and develop a product:

   a. Service providers
   b. Retailers
   c. *Manufacturers**
   d. Wholesalers

3. Music, sports, and historical attractions are examples of which type of assets?

   a. *Cultural assets**
   b. Entrepreneurial assets
   c. Social assets
   d. Human assets

Constructed-response questions

1. What are the different business types that make up the supply chain?

Manufacturers: Manufacturing firms take raw materials and develop a product. Some firms focus solely on raw materials while other manufacturers take already developed products and serve as assemblers of even more complex products.

Wholesalers: Wholesalers purchase goods from manufacturers in large quantities and then sell them to retailers or directly to consumers in smaller quantities.

Retailers: Retailers purchase goods from wholesalers and then sell direct to consumers.

Service providers: Service providers sell services to consumers. Service providers often facilitate the sale, exchange, and distribution of products between different steps of the supply chain.

2. **What is vertical integration?**

Vertical integration is when different companies across different segments of the supply chain are united through a common owner.

ACTIVITY 1
SUPPLY CHAIN MATCHING

Directions: Match the step on the supply chain with the appropriate company profile.

A. Raw Materials

B. Manufacturer

C. Wholesaler

D. Retailer

E. Service Provider

1. CopperCore is a mining company and one of the world's largest suppliers of copper. CopperCore sells the copper it mines to manufacturers across the globe at a competitive price.

    _____

2. Marko's is a regional home improvement store that sells lumber, tools, garden supplies, appliances, electrical equipment, and heating and air conditioning units to residential and commercial clients across the Midwestern United States.

    _____

3. Easy Air is a company that produces heating and air conditioning units. The company purchases some of its components from other manufacturers. However, the majority of the heating and air conditioning units are produced from scratch in-house, including the production of its own copper coils.

    _____

4. H&C Corporation is a company that purchases heating and air conditioning units in large quantities that are then sold in smaller quantities to other stores at an increased price.

    _____

5. SureFreight is a shipping company whose core clientele consists of electronics and home improvement manufacturers and retailers.

    _____

Activity 2
Uncle Bill, Inc.

Directions: Take turns reading this story aloud with your partner. As you read through the story, think about how Uncle Bill's growing business relates to the supply chain.

Uncle Bill grew up in a suburban neighborhood in the 1950s, a time when it was not uncommon for families to have gardens in their backyards. When he was 12, Uncle Bill was given a small plot of his family's garden to tend. He started selling the fruits and vegetables that he produced to neighbors in his town. Uncle Bill liked earning his own money, but there was only so much that his neighbors could buy. Uncle Bill decided that, if he wanted to make more money, he needed more clients. So he began advertising his garden fruit and vegetables to individuals and businesses outside his neighborhood.

His advertising worked…too well. Uncle Bill's business grew so quickly that he couldn't keep up with demand. His family's garden simply didn't have the capacity to produce the quantity of fruits and vegetables he needed to supply his clients, so he decided to purchase additional produce in order to fill his orders. Uncle Bill's father, who worked as a truck driver, helped his son find small farmers in more rural areas from whom he could purchase the fruits and vegetables he needed to keep his customers satisfied.

For the next several years, Uncle Bill slowly expanded his business re-selling the produce he purchased from local farms. By the time he was 25, he had acquired a number of grocery stores as clients, developed relationships with several farmers, and even purchased his own truck, which allowed him to pick up and deliver the produce from the farms to his clients.

However, Uncle Bill realized that too much of his money was going to pay for others to grow the produce—his family garden had been small, but at least he had kept more of the profits. He decided to buy one of the farms he used as a supplier and invest in additional land and equipment to build the farm's capacity for fruit and vegetable production. After a few years and a lot of hard work developing the farm he'd purchased, Uncle Bill was able to supply almost all of the produce he needed for his customers.

Through the process of purchasing and taking over a farm, Uncle Bill learned that he could cut some of the costs of running the farm if he produced his plants, instead of buying them from outside vendors. By taking the sprouts common to existing plants and developing his own plants, Uncle Bill was able to diversify his plant offerings to the point where he could cut out plant suppliers all together. He began growing all of his own plants.

Once again, Uncle Bill saw opportunity. He realized that people were willing to buy the seedlings and plants that his farm was now producing. It wasn't long before Uncle Bill had a lively nursery business of his own, and he developed this side of his business further when he bought out a local nursery competitor who was ready to retire.

During his time developing his produce and nursery operations, Uncle Bill had the opportunity to purchase some land with timber on it. He originally thought that he'd cut down the timber and make a profit by selling it to a lumber yard. However, Uncle Bill never turned down an opportunity to think creatively, and he decided to keep the timber, develop his own lumber yard, and use the wood to pursue a personal passion: designing and building outdoor furniture.

Uncle Bill already had retail outlets in place through his grocery store clients and nurseries. However, he realized that he could capture a greater share of the outdoor furniture market if he purchased a storefront. Uncle Bill leased a building and began selling his furniture direct to customers.

ACTIVITY 2, CONTINUED
UNCLE BILL, INC.

a. What were the businesses that Uncle Bill started?

b. How did Uncle Bill engage with the supply chain as an entrepreneur?

c. How does Uncle Bill's story demonstrate the concept of vertical integration?

d. What were the benefits of vertical integration to Uncle Bill's business?

e. Although the story focuses on Uncle Bill's success, what might be some of the risks of vertical integration? How might these risks have affected Uncle Bill negatively?

ACTIVITY 3

BUILDING A BUSINESS FROM ASSETS/RESOURCES

1. Describe some of the available assets in your area. These may include financial, social, cultural, human, environmental, and entrepreneurial.

2. Of these assets, which do you have the greatest access to?

3. What is something entrepreneurial you could do using one or more of these resources?

4. What type of business would this activity fall into (manufacturing, wholesaling, retailing, service-based business)?

5. Would it be possible for you to capture multiple steps in the supply chain?

6. If yes, how would you do so? For instance, can you manufacture a product and then sell it directly to the consumer and, in so doing, get a larger share of the profits?

7. What opportunities might exist to expand your business as it grows?

VISUAL 1
THE SUPPLY CHAIN

Supply Chain: The supply chain is all of the steps involved in making a product and delivering it to the customer.

Raw Materials

Raw materials are used to make products. Producers of raw materials make a profit by selling them to manufacturers.

Manufacturers

Manufacturers take raw materials or existing products and develop a new product. Manufacturers make a profit by selling these products directly to individuals, other companies, or wholesalers.

Wholesalers

Wholesalers purchase products from manufacturers in large quantities and then sell them to retailers or directly to consumers in smaller quantities. Wholesalers make a profit by increasing the price of the product from its initial purchase price.

Retailer

Retailers purchase products from the manufacturers or wholesalers and then sell them to other companies and consumers. Retailers make a profit by again increasing the price of the product from its initial purchase price.

Service Provider

Service providers sell services to consumers. Service providers often facilitate the sale, exchange, and distribution of products between different steps of the supply chain.

Consumer

VISUAL 2

ASSET ANALYSIS

In any region, there are existing resources or assets from which businesses can be built. These assets take the form of:

Financial assets:

Assets that have the potential to be transferred into or produce liquid capital (money). These resources might also be used to support entrepreneurs in the form of training and financing for businesses.

Examples include:

- Financial lenders: banks, credit unions, other lending agencies
- Existing businesses
- Economic development agencies
- Government offices
- Civic organizations

Human assets:

Assets that serve as a resource for creating jobs or hiring employees.

Examples include:

- Schools, colleges, and universities
- Community-based educational and job training programs
- Existing labor pool, such as unemployed workers, existing workers, and students
- Churches or other faith-based training programs
- Military

VISUAL 2, CONTINUED
ASSET ANALYSIS

Social assets:

Assets that provide opportunities for connecting and networking with people.

Examples include:

- Social groups, such as the Boy/Girl Scouts, Big Brothers/Sisters, gardening clubs

- Professional organizations, such as legal and medical organizations

- Fraternal groups, such as the Lions, Kiwanis, Rotary, and Veterans of Foreign Wars

- Religious organizations, youth groups, and service groups

- Educational groups, such as parent/teacher organizations and alumni organizations

- Recreational groups, such as sports teams/leagues, card clubs, and other interest groups

- Boards of directors of such organizations as banks, school boards, and chambers of commerce

Cultural assets:

Assets that impact quality of life by providing entertainment.

Examples include:

- Music attractions, such as the blues music of the Mississippi, jazz music of Chicago, Broadway in New York City, etc.

- Sports attractions, such as the Baseball Hall of Fame, professional and collegiate sports arenas, and local sporting team fields

- Food attractions, either regionally specific (Maine lobster, North Carolina barbeque, etc.) or culturally/ethnically specific (Amish, Mexican, Navajo, etc.)

- Historic and civic sites, such as battle fields, monuments, or seats of government

- Family entertainment venues: theme parks, water parks, etc.

- Religious attractions: historic churches or cathedrals

- Art attractions: museums, festivals, crafts, and shows

VISUAL 2, CONTINUED
ASSET ANALYSIS

Environmental assets:

Assets that relate to a region's geography.

Examples include:

- Beaches: resorts, stores, restaurants, and rentals
- Rivers, lakes, and oceans: fishing, boating, and commercial transit
- Parks: food, festivals, and family reunions.
- National parks, forests, and historic sites: camping and hiking
- Roadways: Interstate exits, historic roadways (Route 66), and scenic byways
- Wildlife: hunting, fishing, bird watching
- Railways

Entrepreneurial assets:

Assets that assist entrepreneurs in starting and operating their businesses.

Examples include:

- Chambers of Commerce
- Financial institutions
- Government supported services: Small Business Development Centers, Small Business Administration, Minority Business Assistance Centers, etc.
- Business incubators: buildings where entrepreneurs can start businesses and receive services such as advertising, accounting, legal, rent, and telecommunications at a reduced cost

LESSON 4

CHOOSING THE RIGHT TYPE OF BUSINESS ORGANIZATION

Lesson 4
Choosing the Right Type of Business Organization

LESSON DESCRIPTION

In this lesson, students will learn about the four types of business organizations: sole proprietorship, partnership, corporation, and franchise. Students will play a concentration game to better understand the features, advantages, and disadvantages of each type. Students will then analyze four scenarios and recommend the type of business organization that is most appropriate for each case. The lesson concludes with an analysis of how each type of business organization plays an important role in the U.S. economy.

INTRODUCTION

Suppose that you have decided to start your own business. One of the first and most important decisions you will make is choosing a type of business organization. The entrepreneur needs to fully understand the advantages and disadvantages of each type in order to select the appropriate structure that best meets his or her business needs and personal goals.

The **sole proprietorship** works best for the individual who wants total freedom to run the business as he or she sees fit. The sole proprietor is 100 percent responsible for raising start-up capital based on available resources, creditworthiness, and fundraising abilities. While the sole proprietor takes all of the profit, he or she also takes on all of the loss. If the sole proprietor loses more than he or she can cover financially, creditors can then sell the personal assets of the owner in order to pay back the debt.

Some individuals don't want to shoulder the entire burden of running a business, so they seek to share that responsibility and decision-making with a trustworthy partner. In this case, a **partnership** may be the best option. Raising start-up capital might also be easier because two or more people may collectively share greater financial resources as well as an increased ability to fundraise.

A third option is a **corporation**. When establishing a corporation, the entrepreneur creates a new legal entity. Raising capital is generally easier with a corporation because of limited liability, which means that owners are not responsible for any loss which goes beyond what they put into the company. In other words, creditors cannot recover corporate losses from the entrepreneur's personal assets. But establishing a corporation is very costly.

The fourth option, a **franchise**, is a hybrid of the three other types of business organizations. Individuals who purchase a franchise run it like a sole proprietorship. However, some franchise operations are designed as partnerships or corporations. With franchising, the owner buys a name and business plan that has already been tried, tested, and successful. A franchise comes with the know-how and name recognition, but the cost includes freedom.

CONCEPTS

- Sole Proprietorship
- Partnership
- Corporation
- Franchise
- Opportunity Cost

OBJECTIVES

Students will:

1. Name the four types of business organizations and explain the basics of how they work.

2. Identify advantages (benefits) and disadvantages (costs) of each form of business ownership.

3. Evaluate which type of business organization should be used in a given situation.

4. Analyze the role that sole proprietorships,

partnerships, and corporations play in our economy.

TIME REQUIRED

Two class periods

MATERIALS

- Activity 1: Types of Business Organizations

- Activity 2: The Concentration Game

- Activity 3: What Business Structure Should We Adopt?

- Activity 4: Business Organizations in the U.S. Economy

- Activity 5: Researching a Local Franchise

- Visual 1: Benefits and Costs of Different Business Organizations

PROCEDURE

1. Introduce the lesson by telling students that an entrepreneur has many decisions to make. One of the most important decisions is how to organize the business. Briefly describe the four types of business organizations—sole proprietorship, partnership, corporation, and franchise— using the explanations provided in the Introduction to this lesson. After providing these brief definitions, tell students that they will be exploring these four types of businesses in greater depth.

2. Divide the class into four groups. Hand out one copy of Activity 1: Types of Business Organizations to each student. Assign each group a type of business organization. Tell students to read about their assigned business organization and work together to identify its advantages and disadvantages. You might suggest that one person in the group reads the material aloud while the rest of the group identifies the advantages and disadvantages. Once all groups have completed their work, ask each group to identify a spokesperson to share the

advantages and disadvantages of the business organization with the class.

3. After each group presentation, display the appropriate section of Visual 1: Benefits and Costs of Different Business Organizations, and review any advantages or disadvantages not identified by the group.

4. After students have discussed the four types of business organizations, tell them they will play a game of concentration to see how much they have learned. The game has been provided as Activity 2: The Concentration Game. Prepare for this activity by cutting out the pieces along the perforated lines. (You may want to create a sturdier version of the game by laminating the pieces or recreating the cards using card stock.) The game contains four OWNERSHIP TYPE cards and 26 CHARACTERISTIC cards. In order to make a match, students will need to flip over a characteristic and its corresponding ownership type.

Place all cards on a flat surface with numbers facing up. Then divide the class into two teams. Have each team determine an order of play that will result in all players rotating turns throughout the game. Flip a coin to determine which team goes first.

To begin play, the first player on Team 1 will turn two cards over. If the two cards are a match—i.e. an OWNERSHIP card and a corresponding CHARACTERISTIC card—Team 1 gets one point. Remove the CHARACTERISTIC card from the playing area and turn the OWNERSHIP card back over to be matched with its other characteristics. Team 1 continues to play, rotating players until a player fails to turn over a match. When that happens, both cards are turned back over, and Team 2 begins.

Alternate teams and rotate players until all 26 characteristics have been correctly matched with their type of ownership. The team with the most points at the end of the game wins.

Matches for the four ownership types are as follows:

Sole Proprietorship (card #2) matches with cards 1, 7, 12, 13, 18, 22, 23, 25, 26, and 29.

Partnership (card #23) matches with cards 3, 8, 17, 18, 20, 23, 24, and 26.

Corporation (card #30) matches with cards 9, 11, 15, 19, 20, and 27.

Franchise (card #10) matches with cards 4, 5, 6, 14, 16, 18, 21, and 28.

5. Ask students to return to their groups, and hand out a copy of Activity 3: What Business Structure Should We Adopt? Instruct students to read each of the four scenarios and answer the questions that follow. Ask a spokesperson from each group to read the first scenario and then tell the rest of the class which business organization his or her group chose, and why. Ask other groups if they had different recommendations, and why. While there is not one correct answer for the scenarios, possible answers include:

A. *General Partnership: If the three young men trust each other and believe they can work together, they are probably best off forming a general partnership. Each has a somewhat different background, which means they could specialize in different areas of the business. With his degree in graphic design, Austin could coordinate the web design and do the advertising. With his degree in computer science, Justin could oversee the computer problems division. With his degree in business administration, Mattaio could take care of the general operations of the business, including the financial accounting. There is also equality in their financial contributions to the firm, which is valuable in a general partnership.*

If they do not trust one another or cannot work well together, a

partnership is not a good idea. In fact, it would be best not to go into business together.

B. *Sole proprietorship: Marlin has years of experience in the carpentry field. He has the contacts with local contractors for getting jobs as a finish carpenter. In addition, Marlin's wife has a working knowledge of accounting—very important for small business owners— and is very supportive of Marlin's decision to start his own business. Some may say that a general partnership might work best for spouses, but keep in mind that the accounting function is not a major component of the business; it is a support function.*

C. *There are two possible options in this scenario. One would be a limited partnership. Since Demitri and Roland cannot fully finance their business, they might want to bring in a limited partner with the financial resources to get the business off the ground. If a partnership is formed, the Articles of Partnership must specify the financial responsibilities of each partner.*

A second option could be a privately held corporation. Demitri and Roland could sell shares of stock to others in order to raise the financial capital to run the business. The corporation is costly to establish but it might be worth it in order to raise the necessary capital.

D. *Sole proprietorship with a franchise: Due to their limited knowledge of business operations, Craig and Carol may want to choose a franchise— preferably one in the food industry due to Craig's work with the local health department. A franchise would provide Craig and Carol with built-in expertise and support.*

6. Use the scenarios in Activity 3 to introduce the concept of **opportunity cost**. Opportunity cost is the value of the

next-best alternative to a choice that is made. Point out that in each scenario there was no one right answer. These potential business owners had to make a choice in determining which kind of business to form. Ask students the following questions, and discuss their answers as a class:

a. What if Justin, Austin, and Mattaio had decided to form a privately traded corporation instead of a partnership? What was the opportunity cost of that decision and what benefits did they give up with that decision?

   The opportunity cost was forming a partnership. They gave up lower taxes on income earned by the business and lower start-up costs but foregoing these benefits may be worth the gain of limiting their liability.

b. What if Demitri and Roland decided to form a limited partnership instead of a corporation? What was the opportunity cost of their decision and what benefits did they give up with that decision?

   The opportunity cost was forming a corporation. The major benefit that they gave up was limited liability but in return they have more control and lower the extra fees that come with forming a corporation.

7. Introduce the next activity by indicating that sole proprietorships, partnerships, and corporations play major roles in our economy. Pass out one copy of Activity 4: Business Organizations in the U.S. Economy, to each student. Explain that this data comes from the U.S. Census Bureau and provides a snapshot of U.S. business. Note that franchises are not separated out in the data, since franchises can be sole proprietorships, partnerships, or corporations. The data in this activity can also be found at http://www.census.gov/compendia/statab/cats/business_enterprise/sole_proprietorships_partnerships_corporations.html. Be sure

to select the Excel version of table 744.

Ask students to complete Activity 4, either individually or with a partner. Review with students the mathematical procedures involved in answering these questions, if necessary. When all students have completed the exercise, go over the answers together.

Answers to Activity 4:

a. What is the total number of ownerships reported in 2008?

   31,607,000 (22,614,000 + 3,146,000 + 5,847,000)

b. Of that number, what percent were

   Sole proprietorships: 72% (22,614,000 / 31,607,000)

   Partnerships: 10% (3,146,000 / 31,607,000)

   Corporations: 18% (5,847,000 / 31,607,000)

c. Why do you think there are so many more sole proprietorships than corporations?

   Sole proprietorships are easier to form than corporations, so people are more likely to use a sole proprietorship than a corporation.

d. What was the total number of businesses owned in 1970?

   8,371,000 (5,770,000 + 936,000 + 1,665,000)

e. Of that number what percent were:

   Sole proprietorships: 69% (5,770,000 / 8,371,000)

   Partnerships: 11% (936,000 / 8,371,000)

   Corporations: 20% (1,665,000 / 8,371,000)

f. Between 1970 and 2008, by how many businesses did each business type increase?

   Sole proprietorships: 16,844,000

(22,614,000 – 5,770,000)

Partnerships: 2,210,000 (3,146,000 – 936,000)

Corporations: 4,182,000 (5,847,000 – 1,665,000)

g. What was the percentage increase from l970 to 2008 for each type of business organization?

Sole proprietorships: 292% (22,614,000 – 5,770,000 = 16,844,000 / 5,770,000 = 2.919 x l00)

Partnerships: 236% (3,146,000 – 936,000 = 2,210,000 / 936,000 = 2.361 x 100)

Corporations: 251% (5,847,000 – 1,665,000 = 4,182,000 / 1,665,000 = 2,511 x 100)

h. What was the total percentage increase in business ownerships from 1970 to 2008?

278% (31,607,000 – 8,371,000 = 23,236,000 / 8,371,000 = 2.775 x 100)

i. In which years did the business receipts for each form of business ownership NOT increase?

Sole Proprietorships: 1991 and 2001

Partnerships: 1985 and 1991

Corporations: 2001

j. Are they any years when any of the types of businesses had a loss?

Partnerships had a loss from l984 to l987

k. What might be one reason businesses still made a profit even when their business receipts declined? For example why didn't sole proprietorship profits decrease in l991 since their revenues declined?

Possible answers include: Expenses may have declined more than receipts so the firms; liabilities may have declined more than receipts so the firms

l. In 2008, what was the average net income for a sole proprietor?

$117,184 (265,000,000,000 / 22,614,000)

m. In 2008, what was the average net income for a corporation?

$168,291 (984,000,000,000 / 5,847,000)

n. Why do you believe the average income from a corporation is higher than a sole proprietorship? What does this indicate about the average size of the sole proprietorship when compared to the average corporation?

As a rule, corporations are larger businesses than sole proprietorships, with more sales and revenues.

o. Read the last statement on footnote in section 3, part C, concerning the net income of a corporation. Would the actual net income of all corporations be more or less than this amount? Why is it said that the income from a corporation is double-taxed?

The actual net income would be less. The reported income is before the corporate tax is paid. Also bear in mind that there is double taxation for corporations—they are taxed on their income and on the amount given to the stockholders. In the case of sole proprietorships and partnerships, the income from the business is only taxed once.

p. In 2008, approximately how many sole proprietorships were there in the United States compared to corporations? How do the profits of all corporations compare to the profits of all sole proprietorships in the same year? Put your answer for both questions in percentage terms.

387% more sole proprietorship than corporation (22,614,000 / 5,847,000 = 3.867 x 100); 371% more income for corporations than for sole proprietorships (984,000,000,000 / 265,000,000,000 = 3.713 X 100)

EXTENSION

8. To give your students a greater understanding of franchises, ask them to research a local franchise. They should either visit a local franchise and talk with the owner or conduct online research. Common examples of franchises include McDonalds, Subway, Dunkin' Donuts, 7-Eleven, H & R Block, Cold Stone Creamery, Qdoba, and Baskin-Robbins. Distribute Activity 5: Researching a Local Franchise, and instruct students to obtain answers to the questions.

CLOSURE

Summarize the lesson by discussing the following questions with students:

1. What are the four forms of business ownership?

   Sole proprietorship, partnership, corporation, and franchise.

2. Name at least one benefit that is given up when someone chooses to form a sole proprietorship instead of a partnership.

   Divided liability, less difficulty in obtaining startup capital, opportunity to gain complementary skills in running a business.

3. Name at least one benefit that is given up if an entrepreneur starts a privately controlled corporation owning all of the stocks instead of starting a sole proprietorship.

   Low start-up costs, very little government control, income of firm is only taxed once.

4. In the United States, which form of business ownership is the most prevalent? Which form of business ownership generates the most income?

   Many more sole proprietorships than corporations or partnerships; corporations make much more income than the other two forms of business ownership.

ASSESSMENT

True or False questions

1. Most businesses in the United States are small businesses. *True*

2. Partnerships are made up of two or more individuals. *True*

3. Corporations act like individual legal entities. *True*

4. Purchasing a franchise guarantees that you will be successful. *False*

5. Partnerships have unlimited liability for the partners. *True*

Multiple-choice questions

1. Dunkin' Donuts is an example of?

   a. partnership
   *b. franchise**
   c. sole proprietorship
   d. partnership

2. Which of the following is the primary form of ownership in a corporation?

   *a. common stock**
   b. mutual fund
   c. stock exchange
   d. board of directors

Constructed-response questions

1. Why would an individual decide to open a franchise instead of a business which they start from scratch?

   A proven idea; recognizable brand name; franchisor support; exclusive rights within a specified geographic area; established relationships w/ suppliers; financing may be easier than starting from scratch

2. Joe has worked as a plumber for someone else for over ten years. He has watched his boss carefully as to how he runs the business. Unfortunately, Joe has little money to start his own business. His friend Sam would like to go into partnership with Joe. Sam has the money

but not the know-how. Given Sam's past
interactions with others, Joe is concerned
about trusting Sam. What should Joe do?
Should he go into partnership with Sam?

*If there is a concern about ethics, Joe
should not pursue a general partnership
because of the unlimited liability. Perhaps
Joe and Sam could establish a limited
partnership, where Sam provides the
money but has no operational
responsibilities in the business. This
should be well specified in the agreement
with Sam and in the Articles of
Partnership.*

ACTIVITY 1
TYPES OF BUSINESS ORGANIZATIONS

Sole Proprietorship

A sole proprietorship is a business with one owner, and is relatively easy to form. The owner has unlimited liability for all debts of the business, which means that personal assets of the proprietor can be used to repay any losses incurred by the business. The profit or loss from the business is entirely owned by the proprietor and is reported on the entrepreneur's personal income tax return, along with all other income and expenses. The life of a sole proprietorship is limited to the time that the owner is able to operate the business.

A sole proprietorship may be a very small business with one owner/employee, it may have only a few employees, or it may be a very large business with hundreds of employees. All business decisions, whether good or bad, are the responsibility of the entrepreneur. While a sole proprietor may not need to follow as many government regulations, as with other structures, he or she absolutely must be diligent about keeping accurate tax and employee records and following employment laws.

Sole proprietors commonly put in long hours of work. They may have difficulty raising capital from outside sources for their business if others are leery about taking on the risk. Many sole proprietors use their personal savings and investments in order to make their business successful. The sole proprietor bears all the financial risks.

Partnership

Partnerships can take two forms: general partnership and limited partnership. A general partnership is similar to that of a sole proprietorship in several ways. It is relatively easy to form, the income generated from the partnership is only taxed once (declared on each partner's individual tax return), and the partners have unlimited liability, which means that creditors can take personal assets of the partners if the partnership does not have enough money to pay the bills. The life of a partnership is also limited to the time that the partners are working together in the business. As soon as one partner leaves the partnership, a new partnership is created by the remaining partners. If there are only two partners and one wishes to leave, the remaining partner has the opportunity to operate the business as a sole proprietorship once all the legal ramifications have been finalized.

Partnerships have several differences from sole proprietorships. First, partners can secure financing more easily because more than one person is able to obtain credit. Second, partnerships often involve people with complementary skills, meaning that one partner is responsible for some aspects of a business (such as sales) while the second partner is responsible for other areas (such as production).

A business partnership is like a marriage, in that both partners need to work well together, take on responsibility with great integrity, and have good decision-making skills. To ensure success, the partnership should have a carefully worded Articles of Partnership document that clearly lays out what each partner is responsible for doing, how the profits are distributed, and the percentage of the company each partner owns. There have been many failed partnerships that have left one individual liable for the poor economic decisions or unethical behavior of the other partner. And since unlimited liability in a partnership means that any partner is liable for the expenses of the whole enterprise, if one partner cannot pay his or her share of the losses, the other(s) are responsible.

In a limited partnership, the limited partner is responsible only for the contribution he or she has made to the partnership, and the other general partners have unlimited liability for the remaining debts. Many people will become a limited partner in a partnership because it is less risky. With certain minor exceptions, tax reporting is the same as for a general partnership.

ACTIVITY 1, CONTINUED
TYPES OF BUSINESS ORGANIZATIONS

Corporation

A corporation is more complicated than that of a sole proprietorship or partnership. The services of an attorney are required to file a document called the Articles of Incorporation, which are then sent to the Secretary of State's Office in that company's home state. The Articles of Incorporation detail the purpose of the business as well as other information, such as how many stocks will be issued and who will initially be involved in running the business. When the state gives approval for the establishment of a corporation, the state has created a new legal entity. It operates the same as an individual adult who pays taxes and must abide by certain laws.

Corporations must follow much stricter regulations (both state and federal) than sole proprietorships or partnerships do. The corporation must issue stock, and those who buy the stocks become part owners of the corporation. A corporation provides limited liability for its investors, which means that none of the stockholders is obligated to cover the debts of the corporation beyond what he or she has invested in the company. Because of the limited liability provision, corporations generally have an easier time raising capital from investors than do sole proprietorships and partnerships. And unlike the sole proprietorship and partnership, the corporation , has an unlimited life span as ownership, reflected through stocks, can be readily traded or passed on from one generation to another.

The corporation files its own tax return and pays taxes on its income. If the corporation distributes some of its earnings in the form of dividends, then the stockholders must pay taxes on those dividends, even though the corporation has paid taxes on its earnings. This is why it is said that corporate income is double-taxed.

Each corporation has a board of directors, made up of a group of individuals who meet during the year to make important decisions about the company. Stockholders elect the board members, who oversee the overall operations of business. The board also elects and monitors the officers of the company. These are the individuals who are responsible for the day-to-day operations of the business. Typically, many owners (stockholders) do not work in, or for, the business.

A corporation can be a privately or publicly held. A public company or publicly traded company is a company that offers its securities (stock, bonds, etc.), for sale to the general public, typically through a stock exchange. Privately held companies or closed corporations are owned by a relatively small number of shareholders who own stocks which are not traded publicly. Many family-owned corporations are privately held companies, where the family members own all of the stocks. When a member wants to sell his or her shares, another family member usually buys them.

Many individuals and partners choose to create what is called an "S"-corporation. An S-corporation is treated as a partnership and not as a corporation for tax purposes, meaning that the corporation itself does not pay federal income tax. Instead, the partners include their share of the corporation's income losses in their own personal tax returns, which can afford them certain tax breaks. An S-corporation is treated as a regular corporation for other purposes, and requires Articles of Incorporation. S-corporations must follow the same formalities and record keeping of a corporation. S-corporations are also managed by a board of directors and officers, however, the board and officers are typically the partners of the business.

ACTIVITY 1, CONTINUED
TYPES OF BUSINESS ORGANIZATIONS

Franchise

A franchise is actually a hybrid, and can take the form of a sole proprietorship, partnership or corporation, depending upon the legal formation. Franchising offers the advantages of a quick startup, a proven business plan, recognizable trademark and brand, and a pre-existing infrastructure. For many, a franchise is merely a temporary business investment opportunity without the hassles of long-term ownership.

A franchise usually lasts for a fixed time period and serves a specific "territory" or area surrounding its location. A franchisee may manage or own several such locations. Agreements typically last from five to 30 years. If a franchisee wishes to terminate his or her contract with the franchisor (the seller of the franchise), the franchisee may face serious consequences. Franchise contracts tend to favor the franchisor. For example, franchisors are usually protected from lawsuits from their franchisee, and contracts are renewable at the sole option of the franchisor. Most franchisors require franchisees to sign agreements that waive their rights under federal and state law. Fees are fully disclosed up front, and start-up costs and working capital must be in place before an individual or partnership can secure the license. In addition, the franchisor will be required to pay a royalty fee for the use of the trademark, and a reimbursement fee for training and advisory services. Depending upon the franchise, royalty fees (a percentage of the gross profits) are paid to the franchisor on a weekly or monthly basis, while the reimbursement fee is usually paid up front before any training begins.

The franchisee must carefully negotiate a license called a "Document Disclosure." The franchisees, along with the franchisor, develop both marketing and business plans, usually with the help of a territory manager. For the franchisee to be successful, there must be assurance that any future franchises do not crowd the territory The franchisee must be seen as an independent merchant, and must be protected by the franchisor from any trademark infringement by third parties.

ACTIVITY 1, CONTINUED

TYPES OF BUSINESS ORGANIZATIONS

Type of ownership: _____

Advantages (Benefits)	Disadvantages (Costs)
•	•
•	•
•	•
•	•
•	•
•	•
•	•
•	•
•	•
•	•
•	•
•	•

ENTREPRENEURSHIP ECONOMICS © COUNCIL FOR ECONOMIC EDUCATION, NEW YORK, NY

ACTIVITY 2
THE CONCENTRATION GAME

All Decisions Yours (1)	Sole Proprietor (2)	Articles of Partnership (3)	Use of a Proven Idea (4)	Disclosure Statement (5)
Brand Name (6)	Low Start-Up Costs (7)	Divided Authority (8)	Perpetual Existence (9)	Franchise (10)
Board of Directors (11)	Unlimited Liability (12)	Limited Government Regulations (13)	Royalty Fees (14)	Charter (15)
Exclusive Rights (16)	Divided Responsibility (17)	Long Hours (18)	Stockholders (19)	Limited Liability (20)
Number of Restrictions (21)	Greater Freedom (22)	Partnership (23)	Divided Profits (24)	Very Little Government Regulation (25)
Easy to Form (26)	Double Taxation (27)	Reimbursement for Training/Advising (28)	Accurate Record keeping (29)	Corporation (30)

ACTIVITY 3

WHAT BUSINESS STRUCTURE SHOULD WE ADOPT?

A. Justin, Austin, and Mattaio have been close friends since high school, and even went to college together. All three boys graduated last year; Justin with a degree in Computer Science, Austin with a degree in Graphic Design, and Mattaio with a degree in Business Administration. All three are "computer geeks" and have worked part-time through high school and college fixing computer problems. Each has approximately $50,000 in savings for this business venture. They have been talking about starting a computer company (JAM Computer Solutions) in their local town to help businesses and individuals with computer problems or those who need help developing and designing web sites. In doing research, Justin found that there are only two other computer companies in their town of 100,000 people, and neither one will do both web design and computer hardware/software troubleshooting.

B. Marlin Hatfield, who is married and 27, just completed his fifth year as a journeyman carpenter with John Casey Homebuilders, a small homebuilder 25 miles from his hometown. Marlin has just received an inheritance of $100,000 from his favorite aunt. During the past five years, Marlin has been able to purchase many of the tools and equipment that he needs to be a good finish carpenter. He has not been satisfied working for John the past couple of years and has talked with his wife about starting his own business (M and K Fine Carpentry). Marlin's wife, Katherine, agrees that in order to be happy, Marlin may want to open his own business. She fully supports Marlin. Katherine graduated from the local university with a degree in accounting and works for a local accounting firm.

C. Demitri and Roland have decided to combine their talents and open a competitive Cheer and Dance business. Demitri's expertise is the business side. He has a degree in Business Administration with a minor in Entrepreneurship; while Roland has a degree in Sports Management and has been coaching the local high school cheerleading team, while his wife has been coaching the school's dance team. The problem is that Roland does not have as much capital to invest. In fact, they are having a little trouble figuring out how they will be able to get the startup capital for the business. Some of their friends/relatives might be willing to invest in the firm. There are no other competitive Cheer and Dance companies in the area. They have found a building to lease at $4,000 per month and expect that utilities and water will cost approximately $350 per month. Liability insurance has been estimated to be $1,000 per month, due to possible injuries. Demitri, Roland and Roland's wife will do all the coaching and will also do all the paper work.

D. Craig and Carol knew that they wanted more out of life. Craig works as an inspector for the city health department, which involves inspecting restaurants and food service establishments to see whether they are operating according to local laws. Carol worked as an insurance agent for the first 10 years of their marriage and is a stay-at-home mom. Their home is paid for and their oldest daughter received scholarships to attend their local state university. Their son Charles is a senior in high school. Neither Craig nor Carol has much experience in owning or operating a small business, yet this is what they want to do when their son graduates from high school. They have been frugal and have saved over $200,000 for this venture. Craig will not be quitting his job for a while. This will leave Carol with the responsibility of running the business.

Activity 3, Continued
What Business Structure Should We Adopt?

Questions:

Which scenario did your group read?

Which business organization would you choose?

What are the advantages of this choice?

What are the disadvantages of this choice?

ACTIVITY 4
BUSINESS ORGANIZATIONS IN THE U.S. ECONOMY

Table 744. Number of Tax Returns, Receipts, and Net Income by Type of Business: 1990 to 2008
[14,783 represents 14,783,000. Covers active enterprises only.
Figures are estimates based on sample of unaudited tax returns; see Appendix III]

Item	Number of returns (1,000)			Business receipts[1] (bil. dol.)			Net income (less loss)[2] (bil. dol.)		
	Nonfarm proprietor-ships	Partner-ships	Corpora-tions	Nonfarm proprietor-ships	Partner-ships	Corpora-tions	Nonfarm proprietor-ships	Partner-ships	Corpora-tions
1990	14,783	1,554	3,717	731	541	10,914	141	17	371
1991	15,181	1,515	3,803	713	539	10,963	142	21	345
1992	15,495	1,485	3,869	737	571	11,272	154	43	402
1993	15,848	1,468	3,965	757	627	11,814	156	67	498
1994	16,154	1,494	4,342	791	732	12,858	167	82	577
1995	16,424	1,581	4,474	807	854	13,969	169	107	714
1996	16,955	1,654	4,631	843	1,042	14,890	177	145	806
1997	17,176	1,759	4,710	870	1,297	15,890	187	168	915
1998	17,409	1,855	4,849	918	1,534	16,543	202	187	838
1999	17,576	1,937	4,936	969	1,829	18,009	208	228	929
2000	17,905	2,058	5,045	1,021	2,316	19,593	215	269	928
2001	18,338	2,132	5,136	1,017	2,569	19,308	217	276	604
2002	18,926	2,242	5,267	1,030	2,669	18,849	221	271	564
2003	19,710	2,375	5,401	1,050	2,818	19,755	230	301	780
2004	20,591	2,547	5,558	1,140	3,142	21,717	248	385	1,112
2005	21,468	2,764	5,671	1,223	3,719	24,060	270	546	1,949
2006	22,075	2,947	5,841	1,278	4,131	26,070	278	667	1,933
2007	23,122	3,098	5,869	1,324	4,541	27,335	281	683	1,837
2008	22,614	3,146	5,847	1,317	4,963	27,266	265	458	984

[1] Excludes investment income except for partnerships and corporations in finance, insurance, and real estate before 1998. Beginning 1998, finance and insurance, real estate, and management of companies included investment income for partnerships and corporations. Excludes investment income for S corporations; for definition, see footnote 1, Table 753. [2]Net income (less loss) is defined differently by form of organization, basically as follows: (a) Proprietorships: Total taxable receipts less total business deductions, including cost of sales and operations, depletion, and certain capital expensing, excluding charitable contributions and owners' salaries; (b) Partnerships: Total taxable receipts (including investment income except capital gains) less deductions, including cost of sales and operations and certain payments to partners, excluding charitable contributions, oil and gas depletion, and certain capital expensing; (c) Corporations: Total taxable receipts (including investment income, capital gains, and income from foreign subsidiaries deemed received for tax purposes, except for S corporations) less business deductions, including cost of sales and operations, depletion, certain capital expensing, and officers' compensation excluding S corporation charitable contributions and investment expenses; net income is before income tax.

Source: U.S. Internal Revenue Service, Statistics of Income, various publications.

a. What is the total number of ownerships reported in 2008? _____

b. Of that number, what percent were

   Sole proprietorships: _____

   Partnerships: _____

   Corporations: _____

c. Why do you think there are so many more sole proprietorships than corporations?

   _____

   _____

Activity 4, Continued
Business Organizations in the U.S. Economy

d. What was the total number of businesses owned in 1970? _____

e. Of that number, what percent were

    Sole proprietorships: _____

    Partnerships: _____

    Corporations: _____

f. Between 1970 and 2008, by how many businesses did each business type increase?

    Sole proprietorships: _____

    Partnerships: _____

    Corporations: _____

g. What was the percentage increase from 1970 to 2008 for each type of business organization?

    Sole proprietorships: _____

    Partnerships: _____

    Corporations: _____

h. What was the total percentage increase in business ownerships from 1970 to 2008?

    _____

i. In which years did the business receipts for each form of business ownership NOT increase?

    Sole Proprietorships: _____

    Partnerships: _____

    Corporations: _____

j. Are they any years when any of the types of businesses had a loss? _____

k. What might be one reason businesses still made a profit even when their business receipts declined? For example why didn't sole proprietorship profits decrease in 1991 since their revenues declined? _____

    _____

l. In 2008, what was the average net income for a sole proprietor? _____

m. In 2008, what was the average net income for a corporation? _____

ACTIVITY 4, CONTINUED
BUSINESS ORGANIZATIONS IN THE U.S. ECONOMY

n. Why do you believe the average income from a corporation is higher than a sole proprietorship? What does this indicate about the average size of the sole proprietorship when compared to the average corporation? _____

_____

_____

o. Read the last statement in the footnote of section 3, Part C, concerning the net income of a corporation. Would the actual net income of all corporations be more or less than this amount? Why is it said that the income from a corporation is double-taxed? _____

_____

_____

p. In 2008, approximately how many sole proprietorships were there in the United States compared to corporations? How do the profits of all corporations compare to the profits of all sole proprietorships in the same year? Put your answer for both questions in percentage terms.

_____

_____

_____

ACTIVITY 5
RESEARCHING A LOCAL FRANCHISE

1. Name of company _____

2. Location of parent company _____

3. Founder of parent company _____

4. Year company was founded _____

5. Current President/CEO of parent company _____

6. What are the initial startup costs? _____

7. How many franchises are located in your City _____ State _____ Nation _____ World _____

8. What are the royalty fees associated with this franchise? _____

9. How often are royalty fees paid? _____

10. What is the cost for a building/lease? _____

11. What is the cost for equipment? _____

12. What is the cost for supplies? _____

13. What is the franchisee net worth requirement (total assets – total liabilities)?

    _____

14. What is the franchisee liquidity requirement? (Total amount of cash in checking/savings/stocks, etc.)

    _____

ACTIVITY 5, CONTINUED
RESEARCHING A LOCAL FRANCHISE

15. Are there any prescribed vendors? _____

16. How many employees are required to operate the business? _____

17. Are there fees for national and local advertising? _____

18. Are you allowed to advertise locally? _____

19. Other Historical information.

    _____

    _____

VISUAL 1
BENEFITS AND COSTS OF DIFFERENT BUSINESS ORGANIZATIONS

Sole Proprietorship	
Advantages (Benefits)	Disadvantages (Costs)
• All business decisions are the owner's • Low start-up costs • All profits go to the owner • Greater freedom • Very little government control • Income taxes once	• Unlimited liability • Long working hours • Difficult to obtain financial capital • All business decisions are the owner's • Limited life span

Partnership	
Advantages (Benefits)	Disadvantages (Costs)
• Easy to form • Low start-up costs • Divided liability • Easier to obtain financial capital • Opportunity to gain complementary skills • Income taxes once	• Unlimited liability (in a general partnership) • Divided authority • Divided profits • Can be difficult to find the right partner • Potential disagreements among partners • Limited life span

VISUAL 1, CONTINUED

BENEFITS AND COSTS OF DIFFERENT BUSINESS ORGANIZATIONS

Corporation	
Advantages (Benefits)	Disadvantages (Costs)
• Limited liability • Specialized managerial functions • Easier to raise financial capital • Perpetual existence • Freely transferable shares of stock	• Greater government regulation • Expensive to organize • Double taxation • Not easily dissolved • A lot of paperwork • Extra costs for lawyers, fees, etc.

Franchise	
Advantages (Benefits)	Disadvantages (Costs)
• Proven idea • Brand name • Support from franchisor • Exclusive rights • Established relationships with suppliers • Financing may be easier than starting from scratch	• Restrictions from franchisor • Royalty fees on sales • May be expensive to own and operate • Stiff penalties from franchisor if business is sold or closed • Added costs for legal and accounting services • Loss of individuality

LESSON 5

WHAT ARE YOU WORTH?

Lesson 5
What Are You Worth?

LESSON DESCRIPTION

In this lesson, students will perform a self-assessment, compiling a list of their human capital skills, determining jobs for which they may be qualified. Using an **income statement** as a tool, students describe all the costs the entrepreneur must consider in operating a business, including the costs the entrepreneur must pay for resources and the opportunity costs borne by the entrepreneur when establishing and operating a business.

INTRODUCTION

Young entrepreneurs often underestimate the value of their own resources when establishing a business. This can affect the price of their product and, ultimately, the business's profitability. Entrepreneurs must recognize that there are many ways to earn an income, and they need to compare the compensation they would receive through an entrepreneurial endeavor with the compensation they would receive through other employment opportunities. In order to be successful, entrepreneurs must earn from their business an income at least equal to the income they could achieve through these alternative employment opportunities.

CONCEPTS

- Economics
- Human capital
- Income statement
- Explicit cost
- Implicit cost
- Accounting profit
- Normal profit
- Economic loss
- Economic profit
- Return on investment

OBJECTIVES

Students will:

1. Define **human capital** and describe jobs and entrepreneurial endeavors requiring their human capital.

2. Identify the components of an income statement.

3. Define and identify **explicit costs, implicit costs, accounting profit, normal profit, economic loss,** and **economic profit.**

4. Explain why economic profit cannot exist in the long run.

MATERIALS

- Activity 1: Mrs. Rigazzi's Deli
- Activity 2: Location, Location, Location
- Visual 1: What Is Economics?
- Visual 2: Small Firm, Inc.
- Visual 3: Small Firm, Inc's Accounting Profit
- Visual 4: Small Firm, Inc.'s Economic Loss
- Visual 5: Where Did the Profit Go?
- One sheet of paper per student

TIME REQUIRED

Two class periods

PROCEDURE

1. Display Visual 1: What Is Economics? and ask students why economics might be called the decision-making science. Explain that the study of economics is the study of how scarce resources are allocated. We all have resources at our disposal, and, for most of us, our most abundant resource is our labor. So we, as human resources, must make decisions

about how we allocate our labor.

2. Explain that each individual's labor has alternative uses based on our human capital, which is the education and skills we have received and developed. Instruct each student to draw three columns on a sheet of paper, writing "human capital" as the heading for the first column. Instruct them to list skills they now possess in this column. Help them focus on skills developed through education, such as arithmetic and written communication; skills they developed through extra-curricular pursuits, such as playing a musical instrument or skills in sports; soft skills they've developed, such as listening and teamwork skills; and entrepreneurial skills, such as organization, leadership and ambition.

3. Instruct students to write "jobs" as the second heading. Tell them to list jobs for which they would be qualified with the skills they possess. Encourage students to get specific. For example, rather than simply including "retail clerk" as a job, instruct them to write "retail clerk at Sports Authority" or "retail clerk at Build-A-Bear Workshop." Point out that knowledge of sports would be helpful in obtaining a job at Sports Authority. Experience with children, such as tutoring or babysitting would be helpful in obtaining a job at Build-A-Bear Workshop.

4. Ask students to name aloud some of the jobs they have listed, and write them down for the entire class to see. Ask them about specific skills they see as advantageous in getting the jobs they've listed (for example, patience would be advantageous in working with children; ability to work quickly in working in a restaurant; accuracy and friendliness in working in retail, etc.)

5. Refer to the list of jobs, and ask students how much each pays per hour. Help students arrive at an accurate wage. Most jobs for teens likely pay in the range of $7.25 (minimum wage at the time of this publication) to $9.00 per hour.

6. Place students in groups of four. Instruct students to write "entrepreneurship" as the heading for the third column and list goods they could make or services they could perform as a business. Students should brainstorm together to develop business ideas for each member of the group, based on the skills each student has listed.

7. Explain that entrepreneurs can use their labor to start and maintain a business, but, in doing so, they can't use that labor working for someone else. This trade-off is fundamental to an entrepreneur's decision to enter into his or her own business.

8. Explain that, in this lesson, students will learn about all of the costs the entrepreneur must consider when entering business, including the opportunity cost of his or her labor. Define opportunity cost as the next best alternative when a decision is made.

9. Display Visual 2: Small Firm, Inc. and explain that this is a simple income statement for Small Firm, Inc., which records the firm's income and expenses, and its profit or loss, for a one-year period. In this time period, the firm had $100,000 in revenue. Its expenses totaled $70,000. After subtracting expenses from revenue, the firm is showing a profit of $30,000 – or is it?

10. Display Visual 3: Small Firm, Inc.'s Accounting Profit, and explain that the profit the firm is showing is referred to as accounting profit. Accounting profit is the amount of money left after all explicit costs have been deducted from the firm's revenue. Explicit costs are the costs of resources the firm buys from its suppliers.

11. Display Visual 4: Small Firm, Inc.'s Economic Loss. Explain that there is another type of cost that the entrepreneur needs to take into consideration – implicit costs. Implicit costs are the costs of resources owned by the entrepreneur and contributed to the business. One implicit cost is normal profit. Normal profit is the

return the entrepreneur expects to receive from his or her business as compensation for operating the business rather than spending his or her time in some other endeavor. In short, normal profit compensates the entrepreneur for his or her labor and entrepreneurial activity.

12. Explain that the entrepreneur has career options. He or she could be operating a different business or could be working for someone else. In any other work, he or she would be paid, and the entrepreneur certainly expects to be paid in the entrepreneurial venture, in the form of profit. Provide this scenario: The accountant for Small Firm, Inc., reported profit of $30,000. That seems like very good news. However, this entrepreneur left a job that paid $60,000 annually in order to start Small Firm, Inc. This entrepreneur is not earning normal profit, which would be $60,000.

13. Explain that during the start-up phase of a business, the entrepreneur might forgo normal profit, recognizing that it can take time for a business to become established and profitable. However, in most cases, after the start-up phase, entrepreneurs expect to earn at least what they would be able to earn in an alternative endeavor.

14. Return to Visual 4. Point out that normal profit is a cost of doing business. It is an implicit cost. If the owner of Small Firm, Inc. deducts all explicit costs (rent, materials, labor) and all implicit costs (normal profit) from revenue, he or she will find the firm is actually experiencing a loss. This loss is referred to as an economic loss.

15. Remind students that when explicit costs alone are deducted from revenue, the resulting number is referred to as accounting profit. However, when explicit costs and implicit costs are deducted from revenue, the resulting number is referred to as economic profit, if the number is

positive, or economic loss, if the number is negative. Ask students the following questions, and discuss their answers as a class:

a. What could the owner of this business do to reach normal profit?

Increase revenue or decrease explicit costs

b. If the entrepreneur were able to increase revenue to $120,000, would he or she experience economic profit or economic loss?

Economic loss

c. If the entrepreneur were able to increase revenue to $150,000, would he or she experience economic profit or economic loss?

Economic profit

d. How much economic profit would the business earn if revenue were $150,000?

$20,000

16. Explain that entrepreneurs hope to cover all explicit and implicit costs. Economic profit is above and beyond the expectations of entrepreneurs.

17. Explain that another way to look at normal profit is as a **return on investment**. There are many financial investments a person could make. If a business is going to attract investors, it must offer a return that equals or exceeds the investors's other investment opportunities.

18. Explain that entrepreneurs may have other implicit costs associated with resources owned by the entrepreneur and used in the business. Distribute a copy of Activity 1: Mrs. Rigazzi's Deli to all students. Assign the parts of Narrator, Mrs. Rigazzi, and Mr. Washington to three students, and ask the students read the scenario aloud. After the reading, Ask

students the following questions, and discuss their answers as a class:

a. Why was Mr. Washington desperate for a truck?

His refrigerated truck broke down. Most of a florist's business is delivery, and without a refrigerated truck he could not make his deliveries.

b. What is opportunity cost?

The next best alternative that is given up when making a decision

c. What is the opportunity cost of Mrs. Rigazzi using her truck for deli deliveries?

The money that could be earned renting it to Mr. Washington - $200

d. What is the opportunity cost of Mrs. Rigazzi renting her truck to Mr. Washington?

The profit she makes on deli deliveries, good will with her customers, future business

e. What are some of Mrs. Rigazzi's explicit costs?

Answers will vary, but students should state costs of resources and materials Mrs. Rigazzi purchases from outside supplies. Some explicit costs include labor, supplies, and utilities.

f. What are Mrs. Ragazzi's implicit costs?

Normal profit, the cost of using her truck for her business

19. Display Visual 5: Where Did the Profit Go? Explain that entrepreneurs certainly want to earn economic profit for as long as possible, but in the long run, economic profit is $0. To help students understand why economic profit only happens in the short run, distribute the signs in Activity 2: Location, Location, Location. Be sure to cut the signs out in advance.

20. Instruct all students to close their eyes and envision the busy (arterial) street near their homes. Tell them to picture the

businesses along either side of the street. After they have their mind's eye view, invite the 12 students with signs to the front of the room. Explain that the classroom is a portion of a town, with the streets in the front, back, and along either side of the classroom. Place one fast-food restaurant in the front of the room. Place one car dealership along the side of the classroom. Place one of the grocery stores in the front of the classroom, near the fast-food place. Again, point out that there are four streets. Instruct the rest of the students with signs to choose a location for their business. They can ask students who are seated for guidance.

21. Ask students why they chose their locations.

Students may have located near similar businesses or they may have located in an area where there is no similar business. If they located near a similar business, they may state that this is what they've observed on the busy street near them. If they located away from similar businesses, it may be because they want to locate far away from their competition. The correct answer is that students should locate near similar businesses to attract customers from the existing businesses.

22. Use the following demonstration to show why similar businesses are found in clusters. Except for McDougal's Hamburgers, instruct all of the students with fast-food businesses to take their seats. Explain to the students that the first fast-food restaurant, McDougal's Hamburgers, just opened. Invite all students to come to McDougal's. Point out the long line at McDougal's and explain that McDougal's is very profitable. It has very high economic profit.

23. Ask students what an entrepreneur observing this profitable company might do. *(An entrepreneur might establish a similar business nearby.)* Invite another fast-food business to locate near McDougal's. Have students line up at their restaurant of choice. Point out that

the new restaurant is earning economic profit. Point out that McDougal's is also earning economic profit, but not as much as before.

24. Invite another fast-food restaurant to locate nearby, and, once again, invite students to choose restaurants. Explain that as new businesses enter this market, the economic profit is diluted among all of the businesses until, finally, no economic profit is available. Explain that the businesses will remain in business as long as they cover their normal profit. Economic profit goes to zero in the long run.

25. Explain that an old adage in business is "Location, Location, Location." This saying makes the point that having a good location is essential to business success, particularly in retail businesses. Similar businesses locate near one another because of the potential for economic profit.

26. Explain that this happens with all businesses, not just retail establishments. Smart phones, electronic tablets, GPS systems are examples where one company entered the market, earned economic profit, and then was followed by other companies selling similar products.

CLOSURE

Summarize the lesson by discussing the following questions with students:

a. What is human capital?

The education and skills each of us has developed.

b. Name an entrepreneurial venture from your list and the skill that would aid you in developing the business.

Answers will vary.

c. As an entrepreneur, what would you expect to gain from your business?

Students may mention benefits such as satisfaction and independence. In that

case, guide them to the monetary benefits – normal profit.

d. What is another term for return on investment?

Normal profit

e. What is opportunity cost?

The next best alternative that is given up when a decision is made.

f. In what way is normal profit an opportunity cost?

The entrepreneur could be compensated in another endeavor. The entrepreneur must receive from the business the amount of money he or she would receive in any other endeavor.

g. What are explicit costs?

The costs of resources the firm buys from its suppliers.

h. What are some examples of explicit costs?

Rent, materials, labor

i. What are implicit costs?

The costs of resources owned by the entrepreneur and contributed to the business

j. What are examples of implicit costs?

Normal profit; resources owned by the firm such as a truck

k. What is accounting profit?

The amount of money left after all explicit costs have been deducted from the firm's revenue.

l. What is the difference between accounting profit and economic profit?

Accounting profit considers only explicit costs; economic profit considers both explicit and implicit costs.

m. After explicit costs and implicit costs are deducted from revenue, is the result always positive?

No

n. What is a negative result referred to as?

Economic loss

o. What must the entrepreneur do to eliminate economic loss?

Raise revenue, decrease costs, or both

p. Why can't a firm earn economic profit indefinitely?

Competition eliminates economic profit in the long run.

ASSESSMENT

Multiple-choice questions

1. What are explicit costs?

   a. *The costs of resources the firm buys from its suppliers**
   b. The costs of resources owned by the entrepreneur and contributed to the business
   c. The next best alternative that is given up when a decision is made

2. What is economic profit?

   a. The amount of money left after all explicit costs have been deducted from the firm's revenue
   b. *The amount of money left after all explicit costs and implicit costs have been deducted from the firm's revenue**
   c. The amount of money left after all implicit costs have been deducted from the firm's revenue

Constructed-response questions

1. Why is it important for the entrepreneur to seek normal profit when establishing a business.

   It is important that an entrepreneur consider the value of his/her time, effort, and other opportunities when establishing a business.

2. Create an income statement based on the following data: $130,000 in revenue, $20,000 in rent, $60,000 in labor, $15,000 in materials. The entrepreneur left a job that paid $50,000 annually to start the business. Label the explicit and implicit costs, accounting profit and normal profit, and indicate the amount of the business's economic profit or loss.

   Revenue, Rent, and Labor should be labeled as explicit costs, accounting profit is $35,000 and normal profit is $50,000. Normal profit should be labeled as an implicit cost. The business ran an economic loss of $15,000.

ACTIVITY 1
MRS. RIGAZZI'S DELI

Narrator:	Mrs. Rigazzi owns a very popular deli. She can hardly keep up with the lunch crowd. She offers both dine-in facilities and take-out, but one of her most appreciated services is sandwich delivery. Mrs. Rigazzi owns a refrigerated truck and estimates that having the truck to make deliveries earns an average of $100 in profit each day.
	One early morning, Mr. Washington, the florist across the street, burst frantically into the deli.
Mr. Washington:	Mrs. Rigazzi, I need your help!
Mrs. Rigazzi:	What's the problem, Mr. Washington?
Mr. Washington:	My truck broke down. The dealer said it will take two weeks to get the parts, and another couple of days to get it working. The dealer doesn't have a rental truck, and I can't find a single refrigerated truck available for rent in this entire city. How can I deliver flowers if I don't have a refrigerated truck? What am I going to do?
Narrator:	Mrs. Rigazzi certainly sympathized with Mr. Washington. After all, 95 percent of his business is floral delivery.
Mrs. Rigazzi:	Gee, that's too bad, Mr. Washington. I wish there were some way I could help you.
Mr. Washington:	Actually, that's why I'm here, Mrs. Rigazzi. I think there IS a way you can help me. I would like to rent your truck for three weeks. I'll pay you $200 per day.
Mrs. Rigazzi:	That's a pretty generous offer, Mr. Washington. So, it seems that I can earn $200 per day renting the truck I own to your floral business or $100 a day using the truck I own for my deli deliveries. There are other things to consider in this decision, but it certainly points out to me that there is an opportunity cost in using my truck in my own business rather than renting it to you.
Narrator:	Mrs. Rigazzi discovered another implicit cost of operating her deli. She learned that she should recognize that there are other uses for the resources she owns. There is an opportunity cost in using her labor for her business, her truck for deliveries, and her building for a deli.
Mrs. Rigazzi:	Hmmm... I wonder who would want to rent this building?

ENTREPRENEURSHIP ECONOMICS © COUNCIL FOR ECONOMIC EDUCATION, NEW YORK, NY

ACTIVITY 2
LOCATION, LOCATION, LOCATION

McDougal's Hamburgers

Taco Campana

ACTIVITY 2, CONTINUED
LOCATION, LOCATION, LOCATION

Burger Delight

Fish 'n Chips

ENTREPRENEURSHIP ECONOMICS © COUNCIL FOR ECONOMIC EDUCATION, NEW YORK, NY

ACTIVITY 2, CONTINUED
LOCATION, LOCATION, LOCATION

Pizza Palace

Super Subs

ACTIVITY 2, CONTINUED
LOCATION, LOCATION, LOCATION

Frontier Chevrolet

- -

Regal Ford

ACTIVITY 2, CONTINUED
LOCATION, LOCATION, LOCATION

Park Place Motors

Save More Market

ACTIVITY 2, CONTINUED
LOCATION, LOCATION, LOCATION

Loo's Food for Less

Best Foods Supermarket

WHAT IS ECONOMICS?

Economics:
The Decision-Making Science

VISUAL 2

SMALL FIRM, INC.

INCOME STATEMENT

Small Firm, Inc.

Revenue $100,000

Expenses

    Rent $24,000

    Materials 16,000

    Labor 30,000

                       70,000

                       $30,000

Small Firm, Inc. is showing a profit of $30,000 – OR IS IT?

VISUAL 3
SMALL FIRM, INC.'S ACCOUNTING PROFIT

INCOME STATEMENT

Small Firm, Inc.

Revenue $100,000

Expenses

 Rent $24,000

 Materials 16,000

 Labor 30,000

            70,000

  Accounting Profit $30,000

VISUAL 4

SMALL FIRM, INC.'S ECONOMIC LOSS

INCOME STATEMENT
Small Firm, Inc.

Revenue $100,000

Expenses

Explicit costs {
Rent $24,000
Materials 16,000
Labor 30,000
}

70,000
_____

Accounting Profit $30,000

Implicit cost { Normal Profit 60,000
_____

Economic Profit (Loss) **($30,000)**

VISUAL 5
WHERE DID THE PROFIT GO?

INCOME STATEMENT
Small Firm, Inc.

Revenue $130,000

Expenses

Explicit costs
- Rent $24,000
- Materials 16,000
- Labor 30,000

                                     70,000

Accounting Profit $60,000

Implicit cost { Normal Profit 60,000

Economic Profit . . . . – 0 –

RISK MANAGEMENT

LESSON 6
RISK MANAGEMENT

LESSON DESCRIPTION

This lesson introduces students to the concepts of **risk** and **insurance**, and students will explore how entrepreneurs recognize, transfer, and share risk. Through a decision-making activity, students will learn how entrepreneurs assess and protect against risk. Given various risk scenarios, students will select insurance coverage based on the probability of loss as well as the amount of possible loss to their business. Finally, students will demonstrate their knowledge of risk and insurance through a role-playing activity, in which they will judge real-life product liability cases.

INTRODUCTION

Entrepreneurs face risk every day. It is not possible to own a business without running the risk that someone or something will be stolen, lost, damaged, destroyed, injured, or hurt. Insurance protects an entrepreneur against possible financial loss. One cannot predict the future; however, insurance allows the entrepreneur to be prepared for the worst. Insurance safeguards the entrepreneur against many risks, such as unexpected property loss, illness, or injury.

CONCEPTS

• Risk

• Insurance

OBJECTIVES

Students will:

1. Understand that risk is not completely unavoidable.

2. Determine how to control risks.

3. Identify types of insurance available to entrepreneurs and their employees.

TIME REQUIRED

Two class periods

MATERIALS

Activity 1: Avoid, Reduce, Shift, or Assume

Activity 2: What Coverage Should I Have?

Activity 3: You Be the Judge

Visual 1: Risk Classification

Visual 2: What Kind of Risk Am I?

Visual 3: Risk Management - Methods for Controlling Risk

Visual 4: Common Forms of Business Insurance

Visual 5: Other Forms of Business Insurance

Visual 6: You Be the Judge - Actual Settlements

PROCEDURE

1. Introduce the lesson by telling students that they will be learning about risk and ways to protect against risk. The class will focus on the concept of insurance, in particular. Explain to students that insurance is a widely used method of protecting against the losses associated with risk.

2. Draw two columns on the board. Label the first column "Risk" and the second column "Loss." Ask students to describe some risks they may have been exposed to since they woke up that morning. Record student responses in the "Risk" column.

    Possible answers include: getting out of bed and tripping on something; getting into an accident on the way to school; forgetting to turn in homework.

3. Now ask students to identify things what they might lose as a result of the risks identified. Record student responses in the "Loss" column.

Possible answers include: incurring medical, replacement, or repair costs for items that were damaged or broken; losing learning time through absences from school; earning a lower grade for a late or missing homework assignment

4. Explain to students that just as they face risk in their everyday life, entrepreneurs face risk every day in their businesses. Ask students to identify the kinds of risk that an entrepreneur might face in operating his or her business.

   Possible answers include: theft of merchandise; property damage resulting from fire or flooding; an accident on business property involving a customer or employee; a bad check from a customer, etc.

5. Display Visual 1: Risk Classification for the class. Explain to students that business risks are classified according to the following criteria:

   Risk can be either *pure* or *speculative*. Pure risk encompasses events that have only one possible outcome: loss. Speculative risk, by contrast, has an uncertain outcome and can yield positive or negative results.

   Risk can be either *controllable* or *uncontrollable*. With controllable risk, there are ways to either avoid or reduce the risk through the actions you take. With uncontrollable risk, you cannot take any action to avoid or reduce the risk; the risk is beyond human control.

   Risk can be either *insurable* or *uninsurable*. Insurable risk can be quantified, meaning that the insurer can predict and therefore cover the amount of the loss incurred by a given event. Uninsurable risk is neither common nor easily predicted, and the potential loss cannot be determined mathematically.

6. After students understand the different risk classifications, divide the class into three groups. Using a copy of Visual 1, cut out the six diamonds and give each team a related set of two risk types: pure and

speculative, controllable and uncontrollable, and insurable and uninsurable. Display Visual 2: What Kind of Risk Am I? and reveal the first risk type at the top of the exercise. Ask each group to discuss and decide which of their two risk types the statement best reflects and to send one person to the front of the room with the diamond that they think is correct. All three groups should send a representative, i.e. all statements should have three classifications—pure or speculative, controllable or uncontrollable, and insurable or uninsurable. For each risk type, discuss and determine as a class whether each group's classification is accurate.

7. Continue to reveal each risk type, one at a time. Be sure that all students represent their group at least once.

   Answers:

   1. *Damage from a storm—pure, uncontrollable, insurable*

   2. *Shoplifting—pure, controllable, insurable*

   3. *Change in customer demand—speculative, uncontrollable, uninsurable*

   4. *Competition from a similar business—speculative, uncontrollable, uninsurable*

   5. *Risk from cyber hacking—pure, controllable, insurable*

   6. *A person slips and falls on your property—pure, controllable, insurable*

   7. *A worker does not do the job correctly—pure, uncontrollable, insurable*

   8. *A natural disaster strikes the area—pure, uncontrollable, insurable*

   9. *Loss of investors—speculative, uncontrollable, uninsurable*

   10. *Changes in technology—speculative, uncontrollable, uninsurable*

   11. *Increase in business regulations—speculative, uncontrollable, uninsurable*

12. *Credit card fraud—speculative, controllable, uninsurable*

13. *Bounced checks—speculative, controllable, uninsurable*

14. *Employee theft—speculative, controllable, uninsurable*

8. Point out that, as demonstrated in the previous activity, some kinds of risk are controllable and some are uncontrollable. However, in a way, there is a way to control even uncontrollable risk. Hand out a copy of Visual 3: Risk Management - Methods for Controlling Risk to each student. Review as a class the four methods for controlling risk, and be sure that students understand the terms. Then, as a class, identify possible ways an entrepreneur can control risk using each particular method.

   Possible answers include:

   Avoid—Don't go into business at all; choose a different business

   Reduce—Open your business in a different location; limit your inventory; follow all applicable laws

   Shift—Take on a partner to share the risk; purchase insurance

   Assume—self-insure (set aside large amounts of capital to pay for losses); hope that losses never happen

9. Now that students understand risk and ways to protect against risk, ask students which method or methods they think entrepreneurs use most often *(reduce and shift)*. Cut out the statements in Activity 1: Avoid Reduce, Shift, or Assume, and hand out one to each student. In each corner of the room place one of the four placards included in Activity 1 that read AVOID, SHIFT, REDUCE, ASSUME. Tell students to review their statement and move to the corner of the room that best matches the statement. Ask students to discuss with each other their statements to confirm that they have chosen correctly. Note that there may be more than one

correct possibility for each statement. At the end of the exercise you should have more students in SHIFT or REDUCE than the other two statements; point this out to students to support the idea that these are the methods that entrepreneurs use most.

Answers:

1. *Enable customers to use nationally recognized credit cards—shift*

   This shifts the risk to the company issuing the credit card, compared to receiving a bad check or counterfeit money.

2. *Permit the use of debit cards for payment—shift or reduce*

   This shifts the risk of fraudulent payment to the bank issuing the debit card and reduces the risk of insufficient funds on the part of the purchaser.

3. *Shovel the sidewalk in the winter— avoid or reduce*

   This reduces or avoids the risk of a customer falling, getting injured, and suing for negligence.

4. *Provide higher salaries to employees— reduce*

   Higher wages usually leads to happier, more productive employees.

5. *Utilize a security camera or hire security guards—reduce*

   This may deter a would-be thief or vandal.

6. *Engage a consultant to review potential safety concerns—assume or reduce*

   Safety concerns cannot be eliminated and must, to some extent be assumed. However, by identifying potential concerns, an entrepreneur can identify ways to reduce those concerns.

7. *Only hire employees that pass a drug test—avoid or reduce*

   This action reduces or avoids a potential employee performance risk.

8. *Develop in-house training for employees—assume or reduce*

   An entrepreneur always assumes some risk when bringing on a new employee. By training the employee, the entrepreneur reduces the risk of the employee performing the job in a way that is undesirable.

9. *Maintain building / equipment / other properties on a regular basis—avoid or reduce*

   Having properly maintained equipment reduces or eliminates the risk of the equipment not working properly.

10. *Increase your insurance coverage—shift or assume*

    By increasing insurance coverage, the insurance company covers more of the potential costs.

11. *Diversify your product line—reduce*

    Keeping the product line fresh decreases the chance that the product line will become stale and undesirable to the consumer.

12. *Check employee references before hiring—avoid*

    This may provide information that makes the entrepreneur rethink the desirability of hiring a particular candidate.

13. *Limit employee access to critical data— shift or reduce*

    Having only a few people with access to specific data limits the risk and shifts the burden of proof to a limited number of people.

14. *Install / update anti-virus software— shift or reduce*

    Anti-virus software shifts the risk to the software developer and reduces the risk of hacking.

15. *Change computer passwords every six months—avoid or reduce*

By changing passwords regularly, it becomes more difficult for unauthorized users to hack into the computer system.

16. *Have company-wide vehicle insurance—reduce or shift*

    This shifts the risks associated with owning and using vehicles to the insurer and reduces the entrepreneur's liability.

17. *Lock all windows and doors after hours— avoid or reduce*

    This allows the entrepreneur to avoid or reduce theft and vandalism.

18. *Install flood lights in parking lot— avoid or reduce*

    This allows the entrepreneur to avoid or reduce theft and vandalism.

19. *Install safe in the office—avoid or reduce*

    This allows the entrepreneur to avoid or reduce theft.

20. *Back-up computers or store critical data offsite—avoid or reduce*

    This reduces the risk of data being lost.

10. Ask students again to define insurance. *(Protection against possible loss.)* Inform them that, over time, insurance has become a common and sophisticated way of shifting risk, one that is critical to any entrepreneur's business.

11. Display Visual 4: Common Forms of Business Insurance, and ask students to read the insurance types to themselves. Explain that these are common types of insurance that businesses must carry. Note that some of these insurance types are only required if the risk relates to the business; for example, a company without vehicles is not required to carry vehicle insurance.

12. Display Visual 5: Other Forms of Business Insurance. Again, ask students to read the insurance types to themselves. Explain that these are optional types of insurance that an entrepreneur may consider purchasing. Discuss why an entrepreneur may or may not want to purchase these insurance types.

13. Once you and your students have discussed Visuals 4 and 5, hand out one copy of Activity 2: What Coverage Should I Have? to each student. Place students into groups of three or four and ask them to determine which type of business insurance should be purchased in each of the scenarios. Discuss the answers as a class.

    Answers:

    Scenario 1: Property Insurance, with the following riders: flood, earthquake, and business interruption insurance

    Scenario 2: Malpractice Insurance

    Scenario 3: Health insurance; employee life insurance

14. Divide the class into either three or six groups, depending on the size of your class. Tell students that no matter how much businesses try to protect themselves from risk through insurance, no amount of insurance can protect them completely. Distribute to each student one copy of Activity 3: You Be the Judge. If the class is in three groups, each case will have one group; if the class is in six groups, each case will have two groups. Explain to students that these cases are real. Ask each group to discuss and answer the questions that follow the cases. Ask one person from each group to give the group's responses to the class. After all groups with a particular case have presented, reveal to students the actual ruling on each case by displaying the appropriate portion of Visual 6: You Be The Judge - Actual Settlements. Wrap up the activity with the following thought: no matter how much insurance entrepreneurs carry to protect themselves against various types

of risk, there will always be an unanticipated risk that will affect their business success.

CLOSURE

Summarize the lesson by discussing the following questions with students:

1. Why should an entrepreneur obtain insurance?

   To hedge against the risk of uncertain loss

2. What four options does an entrepreneur have to handle all forms of risk?

   Avoid, reduce, shift, or assume the risk

4. What forms of insurance must an entrepreneur carry?

   Property Insurance, Business Vehicle Insurance, Liability Insurance, and Workers' Compensation Insurance

ASSESSMENT
True or False Questions

1. The purpose of insurance is to help protect you and your business against financial hardship due to hazard, accident, death, and similar risks. *True*

2. Personal risks, property risks, and liability risks are types of speculative risks. *False*

3. The most common method of dealing with risk is to shift, or transfer it to an insurance company or some other organization. *True*

4. Self-insurance eliminates risks. *False*

Multiple-choice questions

1. The uncertainties of direct and indirect losses to your business property due to fire, wind, accident, theft, etc., are called _____ risks.

   a. Personal
   b. Business
   *c. Pure**
   d. Liability
   e. Speculative

2. Starting a small business that may or may not succeed is an example of _____ risk.

   a. *Speculative**
   b. Pure
   c. Commercial
   d. Personal
   e. Liability

3. The legal responsibility for the financial cost of another person's losses or injuries is referred to as

   a. Theft
   b. Robbery
   c. *Liability**
   d. Assigned risk
   e. Collusion

4. To protect your company from employee theft or negligence, the business should have its employees

   a. Compensated
   b. *Bonded**
   c. Immunized
   d. Slapped on the hand

Constructed-response questions

1. What is the difference between pure risk and speculative risk? Give an example of each.

   Pure risk presents the chance of loss but no opportunity for gain. For example: If you have a vehicle that is used for your business, there is a risk of an accident every time that vehicle goes out on the road. This means that your business faces the possibility of a loss.

   Speculative risk offers the chance to gain as well as lose from an event or activity. Investing in the stock market is a good example of speculative risk. When you invest your money, there is the chance that you will gain money if stock prices rise or lose money if stock prices fall.

2. What does liability insurance protect against?

   Liability insurance covers a business's

legal responsibility for the harm it may cause to others resulting from the activities of the entrepreneur, the entrepreneur's employees, or the entrepreneur's product.

ACTIVITY 1
AVOID, REDUCE, SHIFT, OR ASSUME

Statement Cards:

Enable Customer to Use Nationally Recognized Credit Cards

Permit the Use of Debit Cards for Payment

Shovel the sidewalk in the Winter

Provide Higher Salaries to Employees

Pay Workers' Compensation Premiums

Utilize Security Camera or Hire Security Guards

Engage a Consultant to Review Potential Safety Concerns

Only Hire Employees that Pass a Drug Test

Develop In-House Training for Employees

Maintain Building/Equipment and other Properties on a Regular Basis

---

Comply with All Safety Regulations

Increase Insurance Coverage

ACTIVITY 1, CONTINUED
AVOID, REDUCE, SHIFT, OR ASSUME

Diversify Product Line

Check Employee References Before Hiring

Limit Employee Access to Critical Data

Install/Update Anti-Virus Software

Change Computer Password Every Six Months

Have Companywide Vehicle Insurance

Lock All Windows and Doors After Hours and While Working Alone

----

Install Flood Lights in Parking Lot

Install Safe in the Office

Back-up Computers or Store Critical Data Off Site

ACTIVITY 1, CONTINUED
AVOID, REDUCE, SHIFT, OR ASSUME

AVOID

ACTIVITY 1, CONTINUED
AVOID, REDUCE, SHIFT, OR ASSUME

REDUCE

Activity 1, Continued
Avoid, Reduce, Shift, or Assume

SHIFT

ACTIVITY 1, CONTINUED
AVOID, REDUCE, SHIFT, OR ASSUME

ASSUME

ACTIVITY 2

WHAT COVERAGE SHOULD I HAVE?

1. Juanita Jiminez thought she had found the perfect location for her new restaurant and catering business. She had found a restaurant for sale on a small bluff overlooking the river; the restaurant had a large tree-lined patio, so Juanita would be able to attract customers interested in outdoor dining. Juanita decided to talk to a former owner of the restaurant to get more information. The former owner told Juanita that his restaurant had flourished until two years ago, when the river flooded and caused extensive water damage. While he had made all of the necessary repairs to the restaurant, he was never able to recover financially, so he eventually went out of business. This concerned Juanita, and she wondered if her ideal spot was really ideal. In addition, the former owner informed Juanita that the city was located on a "fault" line and at the edge of "tornado" alley. What type of insurance should Juanita carry?

_____

_____

_____

_____

_____

2. Congratulations! You just decided to go out on your own and open a medical practice to serve the needs of your small community. There are a thousand decisions to make to ensure that your business is successful, but one thing is for certain: you're going to need to be insured. What type of insurance should you carry?

_____

_____

_____

_____

_____

3. You run a small landscaping business employing approximately 50 people. You can't seem to hold on to employees and one thing you keep hearing is that people are leaving your business for employers with better employee benefits. If you want to retain your employees, what type of insurance should you consider for your staff?

_____

_____

_____

_____

_____

ACTIVITY 3
YOU BE THE JUDGE

Case 1 – McDonalds and Hot Coffee

1. On February 27, 1992, Stella Liebeck, a 79-year-old woman from Albuquerque, New Mexico, ordered a cup of coffee from the drive-through window of her local McDonald's restaurant.

2. Ms. Liebeck was in the passenger's seat of her Ford Probe, and her nephew Chris parked the car so that Ms. Liebeck could add cream and sugar to her coffee. Ms. Liebeck placed the coffee cup between her knees and pulled the lid to remove it. In the process, she spilled the entire cup of coffee on her lap.

3. Ms. Liebeck was wearing cotton sweatpants and they absorbed the coffee and held it against her skin, scalding her. Ms. Liebeck was taken to the hospital, where it was determined that she had suffered third-degree burns on six percent of her skin and lesser burns on over sixteen percent. She required multiple skin grafts and spent seven days in the hospital. Her medical bills were almost $200,000.

4. McDonald's had over 700 coffee burn claims filed against it before this claim and was aware that its coffee was burning people all over the country. It had already paid out over $500,000 due to prior burn injuries.

5. McDonald's intentionally heated the coffee to 190° F despite the fact that it knew other restaurants only heated coffee to a safer temp of about 160° F. McDonald's coffee was so hot it was capable of burning off skin and causing muscle and bone damage in just two seconds.

Source: Retrieved on December 20, 2011 from http://www.higherlegal.com/the-famous-McDonalds-coffee-product-liability-case.html

Case 2 -- Who Shot Me?

1. Prior to going on a quail hunting trip on open range on November 20, 1945, Mr. Tice and Mr. Simonson were instructed by their guide, Mr. Summers, as to proper hunting procedures, to exercise care, and to "keep in line."

2. Mr. Tice and Mr. Simonson were each armed with a 12 gauge shotgun loaded with shells containing 7 ½ size shot.

3. Mr. Summers advanced ahead of the defendants up a hill, creating a triangle among the three men, with Mr. Summers front and center. The view of both Mr. Tice and Mr. Simonson with respect to Mr. Summers was unobstructed, and both defendants knew his location, 75 yards from each of them.

4. Mr. Tice flushed out a quail which flew to a 10 foot elevation between Mr. Summers and Mr. Simonson's head. Both Mr. Tice and Mr. Simonson shot at the quail. They were approximately 75 yards from Mr. Summers.

5. Bird shot struck Mr. Summers in his right eye and his upper lip.

6. Two pellets had caused the injuries to Mr. Summers, one to his lip and the other to his eye, respectively. It was unclear whether both pellets were discharged from a single weapon or whether each defendant may have contributed one of the injuring pellets.

Source: Retrieved on December 20, 2011 from http://online.ceb.com/calcases/ C2/33C2d80.html

ACTIVITY 3, CONTINUED
YOU BE THE JUDGE

Case 3 – The Car Drives Itself! – Background

1. Jessica Mundy was just 23 years old when she stopped off at a FedEx mailbox in McDonough, GA to ship a package.

2. She put her Explorer in park, but after she got out of the vehicle the shift slipped into reverse.

3. Mundy tried to jump back in and stop the car. She was struck by the door and run over, breaking her spine and immobilizing her.

4. Prior to Mundy's accident, Ford had issued a repair service bulletin concerning a potential transmission problem. Mundy had gotten the necessary repair, an additive in the factory-installed transmissions fluid.

Source: Retrieved on December 20, 2011 from http://www.allbusiness.com/legal/trial-procedure-jury-trial/12325400-1.html#ixzz1h5zE6cRw

Questions:

Who was responsible for the accident?

Why do you think that party was responsible?

Who do you think won the case?

Did anyone receive a monetary payment as part of the verdict?

VISUAL 1
YOU BE THE JUDGE

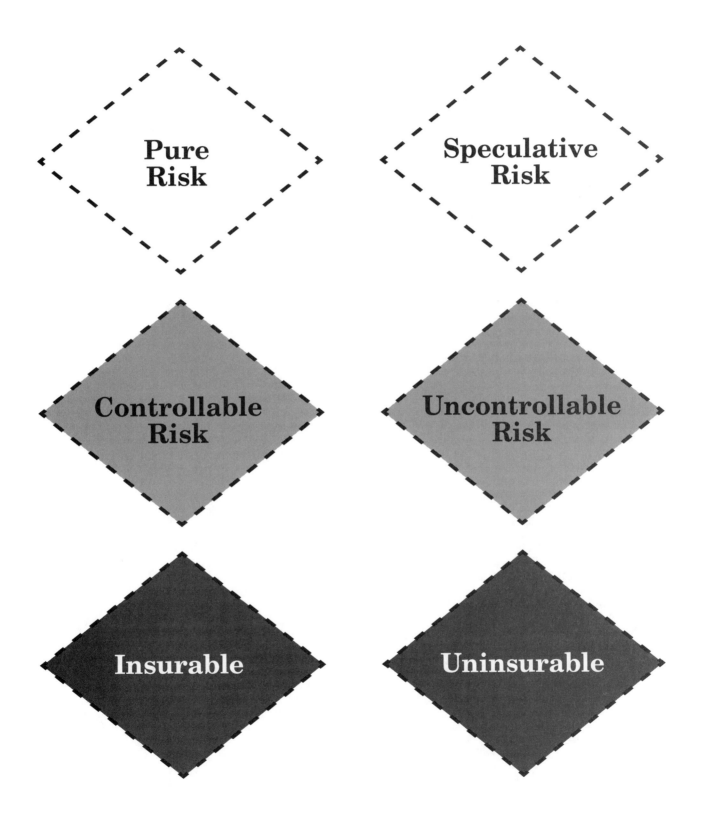

VISUAL 2

WHAT KIND OF RISK AM I?

1. Damage from a storm

2. Shoplifting

3. Change in customer demand

4. Competition from a similar business

5. Risk from cyber hacking

6. A person slips and falls on your property

7. A worker does not do a job correctly

8. A natural disaster strikes the area

9. Loss of investors

10. Changes in technology

11. Increases in business regulations

12. Credit card fraud

13. Bounced checks

14. Employee theft

VISUAL 3

RISK MANAGEMENT - METHODS FOR CONTROLLING RISK

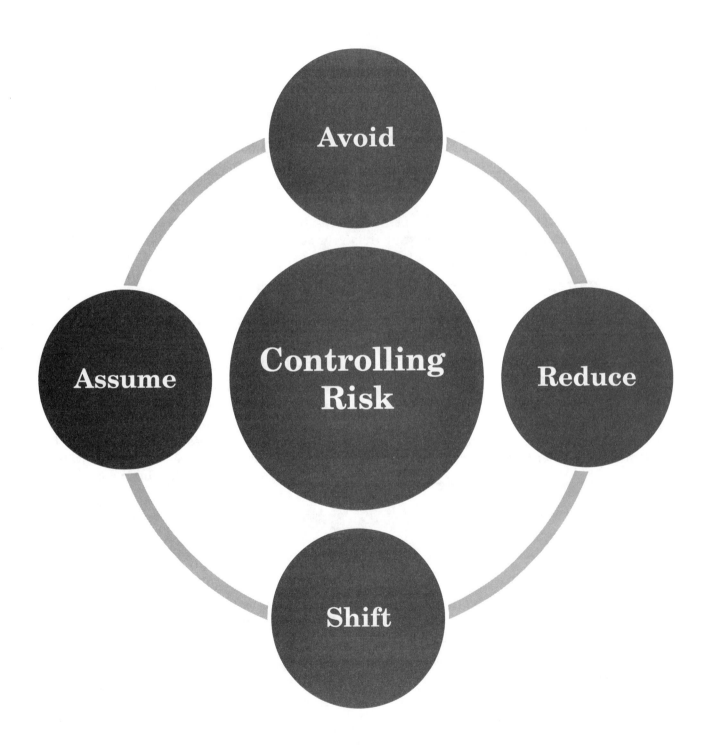

VISUAL 4
COMMON FORMS OF BUSINESS INSURANCE

PROPERTY INSURANCE:

This type of policy covers your building and the surrounding property (if you own) from fire, storms, accidents, theft, and vandalism. In addition, an entrepreneur can add a supplement to his or her property insurance – called a "rider" – to insure against floods and earthquakes.

VEHICLE INSURANCE:

This type of policy covers cars, trucks, and other vehicles owned by the business. It is similar to personal vehicle insurance.

LIABILITY INSURANCE:

This type of policy covers the business's legal responsibility for the harm it may cause to others resulting from your activities, those of your employees or of your product.

MALPRACTICE INSURANCE:

This type of policy protects against financial loss arising from negligence in providing professional services.

WORKERS' COMPENSATION INSURANCE:

This coverage pays for medical care and replaces a portion of lost wages for an employee who is injured in the course of employment regardless of who was at fault for the injury. Employers are required by law to have workers' compensation insurance, except in the state of Texas.

BONDING:

This type of policy covers a business from losses caused by the negligence or dishonesty of an employee or by the failure of a business to complete a contract.

ENTREPRENEURSHIP ECONOMICS © COUNCIL FOR ECONOMIC EDUCATION, NEW YORK, NY

VISUAL 5

OTHER FORMS OF BUSINESS INSURANCE

LIFE INSURANCE:

(in the entrepreneur's name) –
Ensures that, in the case of the
entrepreneur's death, heirs of the
entrepreneur will have money to
continue the business

HEALTH INSURANCE:

(for both the entrepreneur and employees) – Provides
protection against the high cost of individual health
care; in most cases, companies pay a percentage of the
cost of health insurance and employees pay the rest

BUSINESS INTERRUPTION INSURANCE:

This type of policy covers loss of income due to fire, flood,
storms, or other catastrophes that disrupt operation of a
business. It may cover the cost of expenses incurred by
operating in a temporary location.

DISABILITY INSURANCE:

Provides payments to employees
who are not able to work for an
extended period of time due to
illness or injury.

**EMPLOYEE LIFE
INSURANCE:**

Ensures that, in the case of the
employee's death, heirs of the
employee will have money to offset
the loss of a wage-earner in the
household

VISUAL 6
YOU BE THE JUDGE – ACTUAL SETTLEMENTS

Case 1 – McDonalds and Hot Coffee

Though there was a warning on the coffee cup, the jury decided that the warning was neither large enough nor sufficient, and after careful deliberation, the jury found McDonald's liable because the jury believed that McDonald's had engaged in willful, reckless, and malicious conduct. The jurors rendered a punitive damage award of $2.7 million against McDonald's, approximately the equivalent of just two days of coffee sales. The jurors apparently arrived at this figure from Morgan's suggestion to penalize McDonald's for one or two days' worth of coffee revenues, which were about $1.35 million per day. The judge reduced punitive damages to $480,000, three times the compensatory amount, for a total of $640,000. The decision was appealed by both McDonald's and Ms. Liebeck in December 1994, but the parties settled out of court for an undisclosed amount less than $600,000.

Case 2 – Who Shot Me?

The trial court found that Mr. Tice and Mr. Simonson were negligent (i.e., that when they discharged their weapons they did not do so with ordinary prudence), and that Mr. Summers was not contributory negligent.

Having determined that both defendants had been negligent the court then decided that justice required that the burden of proving which of the defendants had caused either or both of plaintiff's injuries be shifted to the defendants, so either could absolve himself. As such it would be impossible for the plaintiff to show which of the two negligent actors had caused his harm.

Case 3 – The Car Drives Itself!

After eight days of trial, jurors awarded Mundy $30 million in punitive damages and $9 million in compensatory damages. Her husband, who became her caretaker following the accident, received $1 million.

FINANCING THE ENTERPRISE

LESSON 7
FINANCING THE ENTERPRISE

LESSON DESCRIPTION

In this lesson, students will learn about several different options for funding business enterprises, including family lending, traditional bank loans, and microfinance programs. Through an introductory case study in family lending, students will become familiar with the concepts of start-up funding, loans, credit, and debt as well as the two main types of business financing: debt financing and equity financing. Students will then engage in a role-play exercise in which they use their knowledge of different financing options to recommend a course of action to an entrepreneur based on the information he or she provides about his or her business. Finally, students will test their resourcefulness by thinking of creative ways to "bootstrap" their way into business without seeking external financing.

INTRODUCTION

Entrepreneurs need money to start a business. Money provides the spark that brings business ideas to life and serves as the fuel that keeps businesses going. However, as we all know, money doesn't grow on trees. Without an initial source of money, entrepreneurs find that starting a new business is challenging at best. While many entrepreneurs use personal savings to self-finance their new businesses, **debt financing** and **equity financing** are two ways that entrepreneurs secure external funding to start and grow their businesses. Debt financing occurs when entrepreneurs borrow money from a person or institution and promise to repay the money by signing a promissory note. Equity financing occurs when the entrepreneur trades a percentage of the business ownership for money. This transaction is also known as equity exchange.

One key barrier to starting a business through debt financing is access to sufficient **credit** and the forms of capital necessary to satisfy loan requirements. According to a 2010 report published by the Federal Reserve Bank of Atlanta, 40 percent of new businesses reported difficulty in gaining access to the credit and capital necessary to start and/or support their businesses. Since the 2008 economic crisis, there has been increasingly restricted access to credit and capital. Lenders are less able and less likely to take risks in loaning to emerging businesses because they fear over-committed, high-risk loan pools and loan defaults. Thus, many entrepreneurs have fewer funding options through debt financing to support their businesses. Indeed, more than half of American entrepreneurs resort to self-financing their business start-ups.

However, resourcefulness is a key characteristic of the entrepreneur, and entrepreneurs continue to seek new ways to acquire the necessary capital to start and grow businesses. Innovations in business financing, such as microfinance, provide opportunities for entrepreneurs who might not have the credit history to qualify for a traditional loan or the personal savings to self-finance their venture.

CONCEPTS

- Credit
- Debt financing
- Equity financing
- Cost/Benefit Analysis

OBJECTIVES

Students will:

1. Define and describe debt financing and equity financing.

2. Identify different financing options, such as friends and family loans/equity exchange, traditional loans, government-guaranteed loans, microfinance, angel investors, and venture capital.

3. Compare and contrast different financing options and consider which best fits a given start-up scenario.

4. Describe "bootstrapping" in business and develop a creative business idea that does not require external financing.

TIME REQUIRED

Two class periods

MATERIALS

- Activity 1: Samantha Case Study

- Activity 2: Samantha's Debt Options

- Activity 2-A: Samantha's Debt Options – Answers

- Activity 3: Client Advisory Services

- Activity 4: Bootstrap Your Way Into Business

- Visual 1: Business Financing Options

- Visual 2: Business Financing Sources

- Visual 3: Start-Up Scenarios

- Visual 4: Bootstrapping Objects

PROCEDURE

1. Explain to the class that one of the major problems entrepreneurs face is finding the money to start their business. Entrepreneurs need start-up funding to get a new business set up and operational for some time since most businesses are not self-supporting until several months or even years after they have been established. Many individuals with good ideas do not start a business because they cannot find the funds to get it started and keep it going.

   Ask students: How do you think most people start their businesses?

   Answers will vary. Reveal that, according to the Ewing Marion Kauffmann Foundation, 70% of American entrepreneurs self-finance their new

ventures. Another important source of funding (16%) consists of loans from friends and relatives.

Ask students: Why do you think friends and relatives might be interested in loaning to an entrepreneur when a bank might not want to do so?

Possible answers include: Friends and relatives probably know the entrepreneur better than the bank does and may be better able to determine whether the entrepreneur is hard-working and honest; relatives may provide the money out of an altruistic desire for the family or friend to succeed.

2. Distribute one copy of Activity 1: Samantha Case Study to each student. Introduce the activity by telling students that they will investigate how a fictional fellow student, Samantha, financed her small business. Students should read the case problem in groups or take turns reading whole-class. Ask students the following questions:

   a. Where did Samantha get the money to start her own business?

   She used some of her own money. She also got a loan from her father.

   b. Why do you think Samantha's father required that she put some of her own money into her business?

   By putting in her own money, Samantha demonstrates that she is committed to the business. If she has her own money on the line, she's more likely to work hard to make the business a success so that she can earn the money back.

   c. Based on your gut instinct, if you were Samantha, which option would you choose for paying off the debt?

   Answers will vary, and some students will probably seem unsure. Students should indicate which repayment option they would choose by raising one, two, or three fingers.

3. Place students into groups and hand out Activity 2: Samantha's Debt Options. Explain to students that there isn't necessarily a "right answer" to which debt option Samantha should choose. However, there is a tool we can use for weighing the advantages and disadvantages of each option called **cost/benefit analysis**. Before students begin the activity, encourage them to think about all of the possible costs and benefits that Samantha might face for each option.

When students have completed the activity, walk through the timeline, costs, and benefits for each debt option as a class. (Suggested answers to the cost-benefit analysis are provided in Activity 2-A: Samantha's Debt Options—Answer Key.) After reviewing the chart, ask each group to share which debt option they chose and to explain their rationale for choosing that option. To wrap-up the activity, ask students to raise their hand if their choice of debt option changed before and after conducting the cost/benefit analysis.

4. Display Visual 1: Business Financing Options. Tell students that Samantha's story and debt options give us a basic understanding of the two main types of business financing: debt financing and equity financing. Walk students through the definitions, benefits, costs, and requirements for debt and equity financing. Then display Visual 2: Business Financing Sources, and discuss the different types of lenders and investors with students.

Explain that, while Samantha's father was more than happy to support her in her business endeavor, it can be more difficult for entrepreneurs to get a loan or equity exchange because of the requirements that they need to satisfy. Lenders employ a number of strategies to ensure that an entrepreneur will repay money borrowed, like reviewing their personal savings and credit history (to ascertain the borrower's history of managing money and paying

people back) and demanding collateral as insurance that the loan will be repaid. Emphasize to students that SBA loans and microfinance programs are critically important to entrepreneurs who may not be able to meet the requirements of many traditional lenders or investors.

5. Tell students that, now that they are experts in the different forms of business financing, they will advise entrepreneurs how to fund their new businesses. Students will work in pairs to role play different start-up scenarios. When students are in the role of advisor, they will need to use their knowledge of business financing principles to advise them on how to start up their business.

Ask students to count off from 1-7 and provide each student with the case from Visual 2: Business Finance Cases that matches their count-off number. Tell students to find a partner with a different number. Students should take turns reading their cases aloud and completing Activity 3: Client Advisory Services based on the details provided in their partner's case.

At the conclusion of the activity, call on entrepreneurs from each of the different cases to explain the advice their advisor gave them. Review answers to the cases as a class.

Suggested Case Answers:

CASE #1:

a. *Equity financing. Ana and her business partners have already contributed a significant amount of money to the business from their personal savings. While debt financing is a possibility, the large amount of the loan ($800,000) and the company's confidence in future success would make equity exchange the most flexible financing option. SmartTech already has four owners total, so it doesn't seem as though Ana would be opposed to trading a percentage of the business's ownership* in exchange for the significant funding the business needs to complete product development.

b. Angel investor

c. Angel investors provide significant funding to companies in the early stages of their business development and expect a high return on their investment. SmartTech is a young company that requires significant funding and anticipates doing very well in a short period of time.

CASE #2:

a. Personal savings, since Mitch has saved up $300,000 in business earnings. Renting a storefront and purchasing equipment won't cost Mitch more than he's saved, and he seems confident that his business will make back the money over time.

CASE #3:

a. Debt financing, because Sarah is looking to borrow money for an initial cost and pay back the money over time once she gets her business up and running.

b. Government-guaranteed loan

c. Sarah has good credit, but she doesn't meet the collateral requirements for the banks in her area—and this seems to be the only thing holding her back from getting a traditional loan from the banks in her area. The Small Business Administration could provide her with a government guarantee that would allow her to secure a loan without providing collateral. While seeking a loan from friends and family could also be an option here, Sarah mentioned that she has already approached her friends and family, and nobody has been able to help her out.

CASE #4:

a. Debt financing. Ben doesn't have the personal savings to buy the engraving

tool, but he needs $100 to make the purchase. Since Ben's business runs as a one-man operation and depends on Ben's artistic talent, it doesn't make too much sense to trade ownership for money in his case. Securing a loan for the $100 and paying the money back seems like the best option for him.

b. Friends and family loan

c. The amount of money Ben needs isn't so large that he needs to secure a traditional loan from a bank. Ben has generated a lot of interest from friends in his customized skateboard work. If he asked a family member to front him the money, he could pay them back after customizing 10 skateboards. Alternatively, he could promise 10 friends to customize their skateboards if they'll pay him the $10 in advance. Then, Ben would pay off his debt by providing the engraving service.

CASE #5

a. Equity financing. Mike and his friend Paul are a rapidly growing company and need a significant amount of money to expand internationally. Mike says that they are looking to pull investors into their business, so trading ownership for money makes sense.

b. Venture capital

c. Venture capitalists are interested in well-developed, high-growth companies that lack sufficient capital to expand their existing businesses. Since FreshWax has already advanced beyond its early stages as a company, angel investors would probably not be interested in providing funding.

CASE #6

a. Debt financing. Maria doesn't have very much in personal savings, and, while equity exchange could be a possibility, Maria sounds like she is looking for a small loan that she can pay back over time.

b. *Microfinance*

c. *It doesn't sound as though Maria has the credit history and/or collateral to procure a traditional loan from a bank or credit union. Microfinance loans provide small amounts of funding to entrepreneurs like Maria who have difficulty satisfying traditional loan requirements.*

CASE #7

a. *Debt financing. Karen can only pay for a third of the expansion on her own, and she has specified that she is not interested in trading ownership for money.*

b. *Traditional loan from a bank or credit union*

c. *Karen has an excellent credit history, owns property that she could use as collateral for her loan, and can contribute personal savings to her proposed expansion. These attributes make her an ideal candidate for a traditional loan, especially since she isn't interested in borrowing from family or friends.*

6. Tell students that, while you've covered the main types of lending useful to entrepreneurs, businesses can get off the ground even if they do not secure external funding. Explain that entrepreneurs often "bootstrap" their way into business, which means that they use what they already have to launch themselves into business without any additional money. "Bootstrappers" do business "on a budget" (for example, by hiring as few employees as possible and borrowing or renting equipment) and often reinvest profits back into the business in order to grow the enterprise.

Hand out Activity 4: Bootstrap Your Way Into Business and place students into small groups. Depending on your preference as an instructor, hand out Visual 4: Bootstrapping Resources or bring an assortment of random objects into class

and distribute two objects to each group. Tell students that they will work in their groups to build a business using two objects—and two objects alone. Groups cannot borrow any additional money to develop their business, and they must reinvest any money made back into the business. After students complete Activity 4 in groups, ask each group to share their business idea and bootstrapping strategies with the class.

EXTENSION

7. Tell the students that they are going to set up a microfinance fund. Students should log onto the Kiva website (www.kiva.org) and look at the profiles of potential borrowers. Ask the students to think about which borrower(s) they would give a loan to based on the following questions:

a. How much money are they asking for?

b. What is their principle business?

c. What about them makes them an attractive borrower?

d. How quickly do they plan on paying the money back?

e. Are there other borrowers that you would be more interested in lending to?

CLOSURE

Summarize the lesson by discussing the following questions with students:

1. What is the role of debt in business?

Most businesses have some form of debt financing. Debt financing enables business to have the cash necessary to start and operate businesses. Small business people also use debt after the business has been established to build and expand their businesses.

2. What are common sources of debt financing?

Traditional loans from financial institutions and loans from family and friends

3. What are the two major obstacles that small business owners face in getting loans from traditional financial institutions?

   Small business owners must have an acceptable credit history and sufficient collateral to procure a traditional loan.

4. How does microfinance help businesses that might not qualify for traditional loans?

   A large proportion of the world's population lacks the sufficient collateral, work experience, or credit to qualify for conventional loans. Microfinance enables these potential business owners to obtain the cash necessary to start and operate small businesses.

ASSESSMENT

Multiple-choice questions

1. Borrowing money from a person or institution and signing a promissory note to finance a business is called:

   a. Equity financing
   b. Promissory equity
   c. *Debt financing**
   d. Consumer spending

2. Funding opportunities to individuals that do not have sufficient credit, collateral, work experience, or the ability to demonstrate a positive cash flow are best described as:

   a. *Micro lending**
   b. Macro lending
   c. Venture capital
   d. Angel capital

3. Growing a business by reinvesting all profits directly into the business is best described as:

   a. Venture capital
   b. Angel capital
   c. *Bootstrapping**
   d. Debt finance

ACTIVITY 1
SAMANTHA CASE STUDY

Samantha was sick and tired of not having enough money to buy the things she wanted. She expressed her frustration to her father, declaring "I need to make some money. I want to start my own business!" Her father was impressed by her determination, and he quickly saw an opportunity to teach his daughter some money management and entrepreneurship skills. He suggested that she check out the old lawn mower in the garage. "The motor died about a month ago, so it's been sitting there unused. If you can fix it, it's yours. And, with a working lawn mower, you would be steps away from being a business owner."

Samantha didn't know how to fix engines, but she immediately remembered her neighbor Doug, a retired mechanic who might be able to get her lawn mower in working order free of charge. As hoped for, Doug was happy to help, and he quickly identified the problem: the mower needed new parts. But, as Samantha quickly learned on her trip to the hardware store, the new parts cost money—$44, to be exact. The whole reason for starting this business was because Samantha didn't have enough money in the first place!

Samantha didn't want to give up so easily though. Maybe spending some money up front would be worth it if she could have a money-making business in the long run. When she got home, Samantha asked her father for the money to purchase the lawn mower parts. Her father said he would loan her half of the money if she promised to pay him back. Samantha went up to her room and scraped together $22 from her piggy bank, her change purses, and a birthday card from Grandma. She agreed to take her father's loan of $22.

A few days later, Doug had fixed the lawn mower, and Samantha had secured her first client. A family friend named David had agreed to let Samantha mow his lawn for $20. However, there was another hitch: the lawn mower didn't have gas! Samantha went back to her father and asked for help purchasing fuel. Her father was impressed that she had gotten the mower running again, and he suggested she buy some lawn bags and a rake to make sure she was totally prepared for her first job. He said he would loan her the $28 necessary to cover these costs if she paid him back. Excited to get her business up and running, Samantha agreed.

Early the next Saturday, Samantha spent several hours mowing and raking the lawn. Much to her excitement, David presented Samantha with a crisp new $20 bill. She set up an appointment in two weeks to mow the lawn again. Wow! This would mean another $20. At this rate, she figured that she would make $120 mowing the lawn every other week for the next 12 weeks.

Samantha ran home to celebrate her success, her imagination running wild with thoughts of all the things she could now buy—both for herself and for her new business. However, Samantha's excitement was tempered when she saw a sheet of paper taped on her bedroom with "Samantha Debt To Dad: $50!" written in big letters. When Samantha went to her father, she asked when she had to pay him back. Her father gave her three options:

1. Samantha could pay him all of the $20 for each lawn mowed until the debt is paid off.

2. Samantha could pay him only $10 for each lawn mowed until the debt is paid off, but her father would charge her 5% interest on her debt every time she mowed a lawn. (In other words, he would add $1 to her debt for each lawn mowed.)

3. Samantha could pay him nothing at all, but only if Samantha agreed to make him a part-owner of the business. As a part-owner of the business, Samantha's dad would have a say in the business and receive 25% of all future earnings made through the lawn mowing business.

ACTIVITY 2
SAMANTHA'S DEBT OPTIONS

Cost/Benefit Analysis: A process of examining the advantages (benefits) and disadvantages (costs) of each available alternative in arriving at a decision.

Directions: With your group, fill out the timeline, benefits, and costs for each of Samantha's debt repayment options. After you've completed the chart, decide as a group which option you'd choose if you were Samantha.

	Option #1: Pay Dad $20 for each lawn mowed	Option #2: Pay Dad only $10 for each lawn mowed, but 5% interest for each lawn mowed	Option #3: Pay Dad nothing but give father 25% of all future earnings
Time To Pay?			
Benefits (Advantages)			
Costs (Disadvantages)			

FINAL DECISION: If you were Samantha, which option would you choose? Why?

ACTIVITY 2-A

SAMANTHA'S DEBT OPTIONS - ANSWERS

Cost/Benefit Analysis: A process of examining the advantages (benefits) and disadvantages (costs) of each available alternative in arriving at a decision.

Directions: With your group, fill out the timeline, benefits, and costs for each of Samantha's debt repayment options. After you've completed the chart, decide as a group which option you'd choose if you were Samantha.

	Option #1: Pay Dad $20 for each lawn mowed	Option #2: Pay Dad only $10 for each lawn mowed, but 5% interest for each lawn mowed	Option #3: Pay Dad nothing but give father 25% of all future earnings
Time To Pay?	*Three lawn mowings (with only $10 given on the last mowing)*	*Six lawn mowings (five jobs will pay off the original debt, but Samantha will need to mow one more lawn in order to cover the additional $1 in interest per lawn mowed)*	*No time at all*
Benefits (Advantages)	*Be debt-free very quickly* *Samantha won't have to pay any additional money beyond the $50*	*Be debt-free somewhat quickly* *For each lawn mowed, Samantha will have some money for personal or business expenses*	*Be debt-free instantly* *Samantha can spend all of the $20 she earned mowing her first lawn, and she can spend all of her future earnings on personal or business expenses* *If her father is a part owner, he may continue to contribute money to cover business expenses*
Costs (Disadvantages)	*Samantha won't have any money for personal or business expenses for the first three lawn mowings*	*Does not get rid of debt as quickly as with Option #1 or Option #3* *Will end up paying her father more money than she originally borrowed* *Cannot use all of her earnings from the mowings for personal and business expenses because she will be repaying her debt*	*Gives up 25% of future earnings—she will only get to keep $15 per lawn mowed instead of $20* *Gives up full ownership. Samantha can't make all decisions about the business by herself.*

FINAL DECISION: If you were Samantha, which option would you choose? Why?

ACTIVITY 3
CLIENT ADVISORY SERVICES

Instructions: You are an expert in business financing. You know the difference between personal savings, debt financing, and equity financing, and you how entrepreneurs should fund their businesses based on their individual needs. Listen carefully as your partner reads aloud his or her case, which describes the client's business idea and funding needs. Using the information provided in the case, provide your client with a recommendation that addresses the following questions.

a. Would you advise your client to use their personal savings, debt financing, or equity financing? Why?

b. If you advise your client to seek external financing, where would you advise your client seek a loan or an equity exchange? Circle one.

Friends and family loan

Friends and family equity exchange

Traditional loan (bank or credit union)

Government-guaranteed loan

Microfinance

Angel Investor

Venture capital

c. Why would you choose this source?

ACTIVITY 4

BOOTSTRAP YOUR WAY INTO BUSINESS

1. Spend a few minutes with your group brainstorming possible products and/or services you could sell with your two objects.

OBJECT #1: _____	OBJECT #2: _____

2. Based on your brainstorm, what is the best idea for a business you can come up with using your two objects? How would you make money? Who would you sell your service/product to? Describe your business idea in 2-3 sentences.

3. Imagine that you make $200 from your new business. How will you reinvest the money in your business? What could you purchase that would allow you to grow your business?

VISUAL 1
BUSINESS FINANCING OPTIONS

While many entrepreneurs use their **personal savings** to fund new business start-ups, **debt financing** and **equity financing** are two ways to obtain external funding for a new business.

	DEBT FINANCING *Samantha Option #1 and #2*	**EQUITY FINANCING** *Samantha Option #3*
Definition	Borrowing money from a person or institution and signing a promissory note that you will repay the debt	Trading a percentage of ownership for money
Benefits	• Predictable payment plan • You don't give up business ownership • The lender has no say in the future and direction of the business as long as payments are made	• Money doesn't have to be paid back unless the business is successful • You can generate significant interest in and funding for your business • Others' opinions and expertise may be valuable to your business
Costs	• If you can't make payments on the loan, the can force the business into bankruptcy • Most lenders charge interest • Takes time to pay debt back and some business earnings must go towards debt repayment	• If you can't make payments on the loan, the lender can force the business into bankruptcy • Most lenders charge interest • Takes time to pay debt back and some business earnings must go towards debt repayment
Requirements	Whether using debt financing or equity financing, entrepreneurs must meet certain requirements that lending agencies and equity investors set to ensure that they don't lose money. Lending agencies and equity investors may require: • Collateral: Something of value (often a house or a car) may be pledged by a borrower as security for a loan. If the borrower fails to make payments on the loan, the collateral may be sold; proceeds from the sale may then be used to pay down the unpaid debt. • Personal Savings and Credit History: Investors look at an entrepreneur's use of personal savings and credit history for evidence that they can manage money. • Contracts and Reporting: The business owner will often need to submit detailed progress reports and/or be legally responsible for the success or failure of their business.	

VISUAL 2
BUSINESS FINANCING SOURCES

DEBT FINANCING	EQUITY FINANCING
Family and Friends	**Family and Friends**
Traditional Loans (Bank or Credit Union): require that the entrepreneur provide a source of collateral in exchange for money and pay interest on the amount of the loan.	**Angel Investors:** wealthy individuals whose net worth is certified by the Securities and Exchange Commission; provide significant funding to high risk entrepreneurs in the very early stages of their business development and usually require a large portion of ownership in exchange for funding; expect a large return on their investment in a short period of time.
Government-Guaranteed Loans: Established in 1935, the Small Business Administration assists entrepreneurs who lack sufficient capital in procuring loans by guaranteeing lenders that they will be repaid.	**Venture Capital:** also provide significant funding to companies, exchanging money for ownership in the company; differ from angel investors in that they are interested in well-developed, high growth companies that lack sufficient capital to expand their existing businesses; often look to fund companies with innovative technologies.
Microfinance: provides small amounts of funding to entrepreneurs that lack the personal savings and credit history and/or collateral to procure a traditional loan; one of the main sources of external funding for entrepreneurs in developing countries.	

VISUAL 3
START-UP SCENARIOS

Note to teacher: Prepare for this activity by making copies of the visual and cutting each case into pieces of paper that you can hand out to students.

CASE #1:

My name is Ana, and I recently started a company with three other partners called SmartTech. SmartTech is a very young company, as we have a new technology product in development that is not yet available to the market. My partners and I have contributed about $300,000 of our personal savings to the company, but we still need over $800,000 to complete product development. We expect that the product will sell very well once it hits the market.

CASE #2

My name is Mitch, and I started a baked goods and catering company out my kitchen about two years ago. I've been fortunate enough to keep down the costs of running the business, and I've saved over $300,000 from business earnings in the past two years. However, I'm ready to move this business out of my kitchen. I've found a storefront space with kitchen facilities that I can rent for $5,000/month. I also want to purchase some larger industrial equipment. The equipment is pretty expensive—costing around $150,000—but it will allow me to sell more goods and make more money.

CASE #3

My name is Sarah, and I want to open a small comic book store in my neighborhood. I've been saving for the past year, but I haven't been able to get together all of the money it will take to buy the space for the store. I pay all my credit card bills on time, so I have good credit, but I don't own a house or a car and so I don't meet the collateral requirements of the banks in my area. I have approached my friends and family about borrowing money. While everyone's enthusiastic about my business plan, nobody can spare me the cash.

CASE #4

My name is Ben, and I'm a teenager in high school. I'm a talented artist, and I charge my friends $10 to customize their skateboards with spray paint and sticker art. Everyone in my school loves the work I do, but a few friends have approached me recently about carving designs into their skateboards for a more permanent effect. I recently saw an engraving tool in a magazine that costs about $100, but I haven't saved up any of the money I've earned through my business.

VISUAL 3, CONTINUED
START-UP SCENARIOS

CASE #5

My name is Mike and my best friend, Paul, and I have a snowboarding product called FreshWax. We started making the wax out of my parents's basement in Park City, Utah, but we've grown enormously in the past four years. We currently have our own production plant and over 100 employees—and FreshWax now makes snowboard accessories in addition to the wax. Our line of products is available in most mountain sports stores in the United States. Our company is growing quickly, but we need more cash to keep up with this rapid growth. We're hoping we can pull big investors into our business to help us grow internationally.

CASE #6

My name is Maria. I live in Peru, and I want to start a business selling alpaca clothing. I haven't established any credit, and I don't have much in personal savings. I also don't own any property. I only need about $5,000 to start my business, and I'm willing to pay back any money I borrow in a short amount of time based on the clothing I sell.

CASE #7

My name is Karen, and I've been in business for three years as a florist. I run the only flower shop in town, and I have been successful in growing my client base. I currently only sell fresh flowers, but I would like to expand my business to sell artificial flowers too. I have excellent credit, and I own the store space. I've saved up enough money to pay for about a third of the cost of expansion, but I'm not interested in bringing on any additional owners to secure the rest of the funding, and I would feel uncomfortable asking my friends and family for a loan.

VISUAL 4

BOOTSTRAPPING OBJECTS

Comb

Bucket

Ribbon

Face paint

Rope

Scissors

Sneakers

Sponge

LESSON 8

THE IMPORTANCE OF A CREDIT RATING TO THE ENTREPRENEUR

LESSON 8
THE IMPORTANCE OF A CREDIT RATING TO THE ENTREPRENEUR

LESSON DESCRIPTION

In this lesson, students will explore how earning and managing an **income** prepare the entrepreneur to administer his or her business effectively. Students will learn that income is a necessary step towards establishing **credit**, which an entrepreneur needs in order to procure start-up funding for his or her business. Students will explore the concept of credit in depth, learning about credit reporting agencies and examining the different components of a **FICO score**. Students will apply their knowledge of credit to several scenarios and provide recommendations for improving individuals' FICO scores.

INTRODUCTION

Lacking sufficient funds to survive the start-up phase is often the undoing of otherwise sound business ventures. Money is generally not available through government awards, and very few start-up grants are available from private sources. Government loan guarantees aren't available to the extent they once were. Banks have tightened the credit granted to small businesses. This leads to a simple, albeit unpleasant, conclusion: start-up funding is more and more the responsibility of the entrepreneur.

The entrepreneur must realize that personal money management is critical to launching a new enterprise. By effectively managing his or her income, the entrepreneur not only saves money and builds credit towards future enterprises but also demonstrates his or her competence as a business leader to prospective lenders. While securing funding for new ventures is not altogether impossible, entrepreneurs must be able to contribute a portion of his or her savings to starting the business and present an excellent credit history to qualify for any additional funding.

CONCEPTS

- Credit
- Credit report
- FICO score
- Income
- Investor

OBJECTIVES

Students will:

1. Describe the importance of establishing a positive credit history.

2. Define and identify the components of a credit score and explain how a credit score reflects creditworthiness and affects the cost of credit.

3. Identify organizations that maintain consumer credit records.

4. Describe factors that improve a credit score and list actions that consumers can take to reduce or better manage excessive debt.

TIME REQUIRED

One class period

MATERIALS

Activity 1: Credit Missteps

Activity 2: Assessment

Visual 1: Credit Reporting Agencies

Visual 2: Weights Assigned to the Components of your FICO Score

Visual 3: Components of the FICO Score

PROCEDURE

1. Explain that one of the greatest barriers to business success is adequate capitalization. This means getting enough money to start and run the business. The most important source of business financing is the entrepreneur's personal savings. Even if the entrepreneur provides an attractive business plan that will draw in investors or qualify for a small business loan, an investor's or lender's first question will be: how much money is the entrepreneur willing to invest in the business? Explain that an **investor** is one who exchanges money for a percentage of ownership in the company. By conducting this exchange, the business does not need to pay the money back. A lender, on the other hand, loans the entrepreneur money, but expects repayment with interest, which is money paid regularly, at a particular rate, for the use of borrowed money.

2. Explain that the entrepreneur must have a track record of sound personal financial management to go along with assets that are sufficient to attract other people's money. Neither of these situations can happen without income, so anyone who is contemplating owning a business someday must find ways to earn an income, which is money earned by working in another person's business or in his or her own business. Furthermore, most, if not all, entrepreneurs have worked for someone else before starting a business. Entrepreneurs not only need earned income to capitalize their business but also find that professional experience working for a business is valuable.

3. Explain that high school students have several employment options. Instruct student to brainstorm a list of employment options in their area, aside from being self-employed, and record the list on the board.

   Answers will vary according to your geographical area but might include: waiter/waitress, cashier, sales attendant, etc.

Discuss the differences, advantages, and disadvantages of being self-employed and employed by others.

Advantages of being self-employed: making your own decisions; doing something you like to do; having the satisfaction of building a successful business; receiving the profit from the business

Disadvantages of being self-employed: staying self-motivated to do the work because no one is giving you orders; being responsible for all aspects of the business, including collecting money people owe you, paying your bills, answering to dissatisfied customers and employees; working more than an 8-5 job; risk of having a failing business that affects you and your family's economic well-being

Advantages of working for someone else: having an established schedule; being responsible for your own work only; having pay that is regular and certain (in the majority of businesses)

Disadvantages of working for someone else: generally, earning potential is less when working for someone else; expectation that you will do as the boss says; interest in or satisfaction of work may be lacking

4. Explain that earning an income provides entrepreneurs with several benefits in preparing to start their own business. The first and most obvious benefit is that income saved up over time can be used to fund a new business. Second, developing good working skills is important—people can learn a lot about how businesses work through employment. Third, personal income management (by building budgets, developing good habits through saving, etc.) is an invaluable skill that will transfer to the much larger task of managing revenue generated by a business. Fourth, receiving a regular income is essential for gaining access to credit.

Define credit as the opportunity to borrow money or to receive goods or services in return for a promise to pay later. A record indicating how well credit is handled exists in the form of a **credit report**. A credit report states a person's credit history, including his or her ability and willingness to repay debts, based on how reliably he or she has repaid debts in the past. A credit report is important in helping business investors determine if an entrepreneur is a good risk.

5. Display Visual 1: Credit Reporting Agencies, and explain that there are three credit reporting agencies: TransUnion, Experian, and Equifax. Credit reporting agencies collect information that assists credit-granting companies in determining if someone applying for credit is a good risk. In addition to companies from which you are requesting credit, insurance companies, prospective and current employers, and prospective landlords also check credit reports. You could be denied insurance, a job, or an apartment if your credit report indicates that you are not a good risk.

6. Explain that those inquiring about a person's credit get information from several sources, including the credit application itself, reports from the credit reporting agencies and even account information from the applicant's bank. An additional, and very important tool, is the applicant's FICO score, which is provided by the credit reporting agencies. This score indicates relative creditworthiness.

7. Explain that lenders take FICO scores into consideration in a couple of ways. The FICO score is generally used to determine whether the applicant will receive the loan and the interest rate the applicant will pay. For example, someone with a low FICO score generally has to pay a higher interest rate for his auto loan than someone with a high FICO score. Credit scores range from 300 to 850.

8. Display Visual 2: Weights Assigned to the Components of Your FICO Score, and distribute Visual 3: Components of the

FICO Score, which provides explanations of each of the components. After students have read Visuals 2 and 3, ask the following questions:

a. Why is payment history the most important component?

Creditors want to be paid on time which is probably their number one priority; one's ability to pay your bills on time is assumed to be like a habit. If you have paid your bills on time in the past, you will probably do so in the future. If you have not paid your bills on time in the past, you will probably be delinquent in paying them on time in the future.

b. What is a good strategy to help you make your payments on time?

Answers will vary, but students should state that keeping a calendar noting when bills are due would help them make timely payments.

c. What is the second-most important component?

Amounts Owed

d. Why would Amount Owed be important in evaluating someone's creditworthiness?

Answers will vary, but students should recognize that the greater someone's current obligations, the less money is available for future obligations.

e. Why is it not a good strategy to increase your credit score by closing credit accounts you have currently?

Creditors look for how much credit has been extended to you by others and what percentage of your available credit you are currently using. If you have two credit accounts, each having a $5,000 limit, and you have a total balance of $5,000, you are using 50 percent of your available credit. If you pay off one of the cards and close the account, you have $5,000 in available *credit. If you have a $3,000 balance on the remaining card, you only have 40 percent available credit. You are considered a greater credit risk.*

f. **Why is it important to limit your credit applications?**

All applications for credit are recorded on your credit report. If you are seeking credit from many sources, it could indicate that you are having financial difficulty.

9. Read each scenario on Activity 1: Credit Missteps, allowing time for discussion between readings. As the scenario is being read, instruct students to evaluate the subject's credit behavior according to the FICO evaluation components. After each discussion, call for a "thumbs up" or "thumbs down" vote on the person's creditworthiness.

10. Place students into groups of three to five students. Distribute the set of six cards provided in Activity 1 to each group. Ask students to keep in mind the class evaluation activity and Visuals 2 and 3 as they rank the individuals described on the cards from highest FICO score to lowest.

11. When students have ordered the scenarios, discuss their work using the FICO components provided on Visual 3.

FICO Ranking Answers and Reasoning:

1. *Patrice (715-765)*

   a. *Payment History—Always paid everything on time*

   b. *Amounts owed—Patrice owes $11,000 but no indication is given as to the limits on her credit card. She pays off her credit card debt every month, not just the minimum payment.*

   c. *Length of Credit History—Three to four years*

   d. *New Credit—No new credit*

   e. *Types of Credit Used—Patrice uses*

a variety of credit: student loan, car loan, and credit card loans. She uses them all successfully.

2. *Jerold (665-715)*

   a. *Payment History—Good*

   b. *Amounts owed—Unlike Patrice, Jerold doesn't pay off his credit card debt each month. He has a reasonable percent of debt to limit.*

   c. *Length of Credit History—Not as long as Patrice. He received all of his student loans as recently as last year. He has had credit cards for three years.*

   d. *New Credit—Tried for four credit cards last year but was turned down, which is a negative sign.*

   e. *Types of Credit Used—Handles both credit card and student loans, but does not use not as many different types of credit as Patrice.*

3. *Celia (645-695)*

   a. *Payment history—Good*

   b. *Amounts Owed—Higher outstanding debt to limit than Jerold*

   c. *Length of Credit History—Celia does not have as long of a credit history as Patrice or Jerold. She has only had credit for one year.*

   d. *New Credit—No recent new credit except for the credit card that she obtained a year ago*

   e. *Types of Credit Used—Celia only uses one type of credit: credit card loans.*

4. *Jason (610-660)*

   a. *Payment History—Good*

   b. *Amounts Owed—Higher outstanding debt to limit than Patrice, Jerold, and Celia*

   c. *Length of Credit History—Only one*

year on the older credit card and four months on the second credit card

d. *New Credit—Trying to get five new credit cards within the last four months and only being successful in getting one of them is a negative sign.*

e. *Types of Credit Used—Jason uses two types of credit: credit card loans and student loan.*

5. *Reeta (580-630)*

a. *Payment History—Reeta's payment history is uneven. She missed one payment completely 18 months ago and was 60 days behind on payments another time. However, she is currently up to date on payments.*

b. *Amount Owed—Very high outstanding debt to limit: 100%*

c. *Length of Credit History—It's unclear when she obtained her first credit card, but we know she has a credit history of at least 1.5 years, since she missed a payment 18 months ago.*

d. *New Credit—Reeta only uses one type of credit: a credit card loan.*

6. *Leo (545-595)*

a. *Payment History—Leo's payment history is uneven. He missed a payment two months ago, and he has been delinquent in making timely payments in the past.*

b. *Amount Owed—Leo's outstanding debt to limit is 100%. He only pays the minimum when he makes payments.*

c. *Length of Credit History—Leo appears to have a shorter credit history than Reeta.*

d. *New Credit—None*

e. *Types of Credit Used—Leo only uses*

one type of credit: a credit card loan.

10. Reeta and Leo have relatively low FICO scores, which means that they will be paying more for the credit that they secure. List on the board some of the ways they could improve their credit scores.

a. Make sure that they make payments on time. Keep in mind that payment history is the component of the FICO score which is the greatest percentage.

b. Forego buying so many things on credit since their credit balance to credit limit for both of them is 100%. Whenever possible, pay off the balance each month instead of just making the minimum payment. The "amounts owed" component is the second-largest percentage of the FICO score.

c. If they continue to use credit wisely through the years, they will receive more points for the length of credit history.

d. Do not apply for new credit until they have been more responsible with the credit that they have at the current time. Do not apply for more credit cards at the present time since they may not be successful in getting more and their attempts will negatively affect their credit scores.

e. After becoming more responsible with the credit they currently have, they could gain additional credit, such as a mortgage, car loan, etc.

11. Optional: Students can develop their own scenarios and estimate FICO scores at www.whatsmyscore.org/estimator. This exercise will make them more aware of the criteria considered in the FICO score.

CLOSURE

Summarize the lesson by discussing the following questions with students:

1. How does earning an income prepare you for starting a business?

Earning an income helps develop personal money management skills which could transfer to business money management skills. Income can provide you with savings that can be used to help establish a business. Earning an income is a prerequisite for establishing the credit necessary to fund a business start-up.

2. Once you have established credit, who monitors your ability to manage it?

   There are three credit-reporting agencies: TransUnion, Experian, and Equifax.

3. The information on your credit reports results in a FICO score. What information is used to calculate the score?

   Payment history 35%; amounts owed 30%; length of credit history 15%; new credit 10%; types of credit used 10%

4. Explain how a credit score affects creditworthiness and the cost of credit.

   A low FICO score can result in a higher interest rate or being disqualified for credit altogether.

5. Explain the factors that improve a credit score.

   Responsible credit behavior over time is the only way to improve your score. That behavior includes never being late or missing a payment; reducing the amount of debt to a lower percentage of the total credit available to you; and being careful not to open too many credit card accounts or apply for a number of credit cards in a short time frame.

6. Describe ways to avoid or correct credit problems.

   Always pay your bills on time and never miss a payment. Pay your balance each month to avoid becoming overextended and paying interest.

7. List actions that a consumer could take to reduce or better manage excessive debt.

   Stop spending! Buy only what's necessary, and use the rest of your income to reduce

debt. Pay the highest interest rate obligations first, while maintaining at least the minimum payments on all other debt.

ASSESSMENT

Provide a copy of Activity 2: Assessment to each student. Instruct them to read each scenario and identify the FICO component where the subjects may lose points. Students should provide the subjects with advice as to how they might change their behavior to improve their credit score.

Suggested Answers:

Chloe

Payment History. Chloe must develop a more mature attitude toward her finances. It's crucial that she pay her bills on time; she must force herself to be responsible.

Sophia

Payment History. Sophia must prioritize her actions and realize that no matter how important it is to have a spotless apartment, it is even more important to have a spotless payment history.

Rhoda

Payment History. First, Rhoda should not have been taken by surprise by her balance. She wasn't paying attention to what she was spending. Second, she should have paid what she could out of the money she had available prior to the 15th and accepted the extra interest payment. Now, she will pay the interest payment, a late fee, and her credit report will reflect the late payment.

Ethan

Amounts Owed. Paying off the high-interest card was a great idea but cancelling the card lowered the amount of credit available to him and increased his ratio of debt to available credit. Ethan should not repeat this mistake as he pays off his remaining debt.

Leesa

Length of Credit History. Leesa should be

admired for her commitment to financial responsibility; however, she must establish credit for many reasons other than obtaining credit. Among those who will consult her credit record are potential landlords, employers, and insurers, so having access to credit is important. On top of that, it's nearly impossible to rent a car or get a hotel reservation without a credit card.

Sharona

New Credit and Types of Credit Used. Sharona needs to recognize that many inquiries reduce her FICO score. In addition, she is heavy in credit cards and has reduced her prospects of varying her credit with a car loan. Sharona could have just one or two credit cards that provide her with a rewards program so that she is getting something in return for her loyalty to those particular cards. Maybe she will feel a little better about missing out on those one-time store discounts in the future.

ACTIVITY 1
CREDIT MISSTEPS

Note to teacher: Prepare for this activity by making copies of the visual and cutting each case into separate cards. Each group of students should get a set of six cards.

Patrice has had a credit card for three years. She took out a student loan four years ago, and she applied for and received a car loan last year. The balance on her student loan is $5,000, and her balance on the car loan is $6,000. She pays her credit card off each month. She has never been late on a payment on either of her loans or on her credit card.

Jerold has had two credit cards for three years. He also has a couple of student loans totaling $5,000, all of which he received last year. He applied for four credit cards last year, but was turned down. He was hoping to get at least one of those cards because his balances are up there – totaling $5,000 on the two cards. But his $10,000 in debt is only around 45 percent of his limit, and he's never missed a payment, so he's feeling pretty good about his money management skills.

Celia applied for and received her first credit card one year ago as she was entering college. She regularly carries a $2,000 balance on that card, which is 50 percent of her $4,000 credit limit. She's never missed a payment; she's never even been late.

Jason is a junior in college. He got one credit card a year ago and opened a new credit card account four months ago, which was the one successful credit card application of the five credit cards he applied for last year. He carries a $2,500 balance on the older card, which is 100 percent of his credit limit on that card. Although he promised himself that he would only use the second card for emergencies, he now has a $2,500 balance on that card too. He also has a student loan for $5,000. He's never missed a payment and has no past-due accounts.

Reeta has only applied for and received one credit card. The card has a $5,000 limit, and Reeta has a $5,000 balance. She missed a payment 18 months ago and was 30 days delinquent before she got the money together to make the minimum payment. She is making the monthly payments on time now.

Leo has only applied for one credit card, which was granted. He carries a $5,000 balance, which is his credit limit on the card. He missed a payment two months ago, and has been as many as 60 days delinquent in the past. However, at this time, he's caught up on making the minimum payment.

ACTIVITY 2

ASSESSMENT

Instructions: Read each situation below and name the FICO score component where the subjects may lose points. Provide each with advice as to how they might adjust their behavior to get their credit back on track.

Chloe travels a lot for her work. The mail piles up and the stacks can be pretty overwhelming, so she ignores them until the spirit moves her. She has plenty of money to pay the bills, but finds it hard to get around to opening the mail.

Sophia can't stand having anyone over to visit unless her home is perfect. If she is having company, you can bet everything will be dusted and washed, and candles will scent the air. Last month, Sophia's new boyfriend called and asked to stop by – he was only 15 minutes away! With so little time to get things in place, Sophia grabbed a box and ran around throwing everything that was out of place into the box. She put the box into the closet, and her apartment was immaculate. One month later, she discovered the forgotten box and the overdue credit card bill it contained.

Rhoda likes to pay her credit card off each month. Last month, her balance was higher than she expected. It was due on the 15th, and she gets paid on the 15th, so she decided to pay the balance through her online banking account. She arranged to make the payment on the 15th, but for some reason, the payment wasn't applied until the 16th.

Ethan carried really high balances on his credit card, relative to his income. He had four credit cards: the Copper card had a balance of $5,284 with an interest rate of 17 percent; the Platinum Silver card had a balance of $7,639 with an interest rate of 15 percent; the Golden Platinum card had a balance of $10,290 with an interest rate of 21 percent; and the Palladium Plus card had a balance of $2,340 with an interest rate of 16 percent. Each card had a $10,000 credit limit. So Ethan did the smart thing and made minimum payments on all cards except for the Golden Platinum. It had the highest interest rate, so he made large payments for months and finally paid it off. He was so thrilled with his accomplishment that he celebrated by calling to cancel the card.

Leesa saw so many people get into serious trouble with credit cards (including her own parents) that she decided that she would maintain a "cash only" lifestyle. She buys only those things that she can pay for with the cash she had on hand and, therefore, has never been in trouble with credit. She is also a prudent saver, so she has managed to save enough money to rent an apartment. The landlord told her he will be checking her credit report.

Sharona graduated from college in her hometown of Chicago and landed a great job in St. Louis. She had to furnish her apartment, get a car, and buy a workplace wardrobe. With her Platinum Perfect card in hand, she got to shopping. However, with each purchase, she was informed of how much more she would save if she just applied for the store credit card. So, she did. She ended up applying for 7 or 8 cards and got them all with rather low limits of $500 to $1,000. Then she went to buy a car and her loan application was turned down.

VISUAL 1

CREDIT REPORTING AGENCIES

TransUnion

Experian

Equifax

VISUAL 2

WEIGHTS ASSIGNED TO THE COMPONENTS OF YOUR FICO SCORE

Payment History 35%

Amounts Owed 30%

Length of Credit History 15%

New Credit 10%

Types of Credit Used 10%

Source: http://www.myfico.com/CreditEducation/WhatsInYourScore.aspx

VISUAL 3
COMPONENTS OF THE **FICO** SCORE

Payment History	This component of the FICO score looks at whether you pay your bills on time or have missed payments altogether. Payment history is the largest portion of the FICO score, so it is essential when trying to build the highest possible FICO score that you never send a late payment. Keep a calendar to help you remember when to send payments.
Amounts Owed	This component considers how much debt you have outstanding. For example, if you have borrowed the maximum amount available on your credit card and make only minimum payments, you will lose points in this category. Some people think that it's a good strategy to pay off a credit card and then close the account. They are partially correct. It is a good strategy to pay off the credit card, but it is not advisable to close the account. If you have two credit cards with limits of $5,000 each and owe $4,000 on one of them, you are looked at more favorably than someone who has one credit card with a limit of $5,000 on which he owes $4,000. If you have two credit cards, each with a $5,000 limit, you have $10,000 worth of credit available. If you have a debt of $4,000 on one card and no debt on the other, you are using 40 percent of the credit available to you. On the other hand, if you have one card with a $5,000 limit and you have $4,000 on that card, you are using 80 percent of the credit available to you. The lower the percent of available credit you use, the better your score.
Length of Credit History	This component looks at how long you've maintained credit. There isn't much you can do about being young, but the sooner you can begin to establish a credit history, the better. Begin slowly by opening one credit account and managing it well. A cell phone account or a monthly automobile insurance payment could be a good start. Do not open too many accounts too quickly.
New Credit	This component looks at the number of accounts you are opening and how many inquiries have been made to credit bureaus on your behalf. Inquiries are made when you apply for credit. Those to whom you are applying check with each credit bureau to see if you are a good risk. Many inquires for a type of credit, such as credit cards, could indicate that you are seeking multiple credit accounts, which could indicate that you are having financial difficulties. If you are shopping for a credit account to buy a car, for instance, be sure to narrow the time frame of your credit inquiries. When several inquiries for a car loan come close together, it doesn't count against you because it is obvious you are shopping for the best interest rate for a specific purchase.
Types of Credit Used	This component looks at the types of credit cards and installment loans you have. Be careful not to load up on credit cards – be choosy. It's easy to be persuaded to apply for credit when offered an immediate 10 percent discount off your purchase if you open a credit account.

THE ENTREPRENEUR AND HUMAN CAPITAL

LESSON 9
THE ENTREPRENEUR AND HUMAN CAPITAL

OVERVIEW

In this lesson, students investigate the ways in which the entrepreneur develops his or her **human capital**. By analyzing employment data, students discover the relationship between a person's education and earnings potential. Students then explore the competency model as a framework for thinking about education and professional development, defining and reflecting on the competencies the entrepreneur needs in order to run a business successfully. Finally, students will complete a self-assessment and identify the competencies they need to work on in order to increase their entrepreneurial potential.

INTRODUCTION

Successful entrepreneurs start their businesses with some expertise in one or more of the following areas: managing people and resources, marketing goods and services, keeping business records, acquiring financing, producing goods and services, and understanding the economic environment in which their business operates. However, this doesn't mean that entrepreneurs are born business experts. Rather, they are willing to gain the knowledge and skills necessary to run their businesses successfully.

Entrepreneurs understand that learning is a life-long endeavor that encompasses academic, professional, technical, and personal growth. While Bill Gates and Steve Jobs are well-known examples of successful entrepreneurs who dropped out of college to pursue their business ideas, education—whether through formal study at an institution or self-study—is critical to entrepreneurial success. Indeed, one would be hard pressed to find a successful entrepreneur who is not an avid, voracious learner throughout his or her life.

CONCEPTS

*   Human capital

OBJECTIVES

Students will:

1. Analyze the relationships between education levels, median weekly incomes, and unemployment rates.

2. Define human capital and list reasons why the entrepreneur is interested in developing his or her human capital.

3. List ways in which human capital is and can be developed.

4. Describe the various ways in which one can pursue professional development.

TIME REQUIRED

One class period

MATERIALS

Activity 1: Education and Human Capital

Activity 2: Entrepreneurship Competencies

Activity 3: How Do I Know What I Need to Work On?

Activity 4: What Next?

Visual 1: Competency Models and Human Capital

PROCEDURE

1. Ask the following questions and discuss students' answers as a class:

    a. What are some skills that you have today that your parents or grandparents might not have had when they were your age?

    Possible answers include: writing e-mails; texting; conducting Internet searches; online shopping; using the Facebook or MySpace; downloading apps; navigating a touch screen; etc.

b. Ask students: Why might these skills be important in the workplace today?

Possible answers include: communicating and networking with colleagues and prospective employers; researching competitors; advertising a business; understanding customers; etc.

c. Ask students: If you didn't have these skills already, what could you do to learn them?

Possible answers include: take a class at a college or university, in-person or online; ask a friend or an expert; engage in self-study through independent reading and researching

2. Explain to students that, in order to remain competitive in today's rapidly changing world, people need to update their knowledge, education, and skills. Whether "taking a job" through traditional employment at a firm or "making a job" through entrepreneurship, individuals must continuously develop the skills that will enable them to remain competitive in the marketplace. Tell students that economists call the development of such knowledge and understanding **human capital**. Human capital can be developed in many different ways—a formal school setting, self-education, business-sponsored training programs, and on-the-job experiences.

3. Explain to students that an individual's education most significantly impacts his or her human capital. Divide students into pairs, and hand out Activity 1: Education and Human Capital. Tell students to use the graphs provided in the activity to answer questions about the relationship between education and economic opportunity. Review students' answers as a class.

a. What is the relationship between median weekly earnings and education levels?

There is a direct relationship between median weekly earnings and education

levels. On average, people with higher levels of education earn higher median weekly earnings; on average, people with lower levels of education earn lower median weekly earnings.

b. What is the relationship between unemployment rates and education levels?

People with lower levels of education face higher unemployment rates; people with higher levels of education face lower unemployment rates.

c. What does this tell you about the impact of education on an individual's human capital and future economic opportunity?

Education enables individuals to significantly increase their human capital—or future ability to make money. Individuals with higher levels of education earn more money and face lower unemployment rates.

d. Getting an education costs money. Based on your answers to the questions above, why might you be willing to spend money on educational opportunities?

Education is an investment for the future. While paying for an education now may put you in debt, education eventually pays off through higher earnings and lower unemployment rates.

4. Explain that, since the entrepreneur is self-employed, he or she must take charge of his or her own human capital and pursue educational opportunities that will provide him or her with the skills and knowledge to remain successful. Display Visual 1: Competency Models and Human Capital, and provide copies of Visual 1 as hand-outs to students. Explain to students that a competency model provides a useful framework for thinking about the knowledge, skills, and abilities people need in order to perform successfully in a particular work setting. Tell students that

the first image on Visual 1 includes three building blocks, which each represent a set of related competencies: foundational, industry related, and occupation related. The building blocks are arranged in a pyramid because, as you move from the base upwards, the competencies become increasingly specific to certain industries or occupations. Tell students that the second image on Visual 1 represents a competency model that is specific to the entrepreneur. Depending on access to the internet, you may choose to explore the interactive version of the visual, which can be found online at: http://www.careeronestop.org/competencym odel/pyramid.aspx?ENTRE=Y

5. Hand out Activity 2: Entrepreneurship Competencies, and tell students that they will be working in groups to consider more closely the competencies listed on the entrepreneurship model. Explain that the class will focus on the foundational skills required to be an entrepreneur, since entrepreneurs can create businesses that span different industries and require different occupational skills. However, students should remember that, as the pyramid that rises from this foundational base demonstrates, the successful entrepreneur must also gain competencies acquired through industry, occupational, and management experience. Divide students into groups of four. Assign each group a number, counting off from 1-3. Groups 1 will work on personal effectiveness competencies; Groups 2 will work on academic competencies, and Groups 3 will work on workplace competencies. Students should work in their groups to develop definitions and scenarios for their assigned category of competencies. After students have completed their work, ask students from each group to share their definitions and scenarios with the class. Suggested definitions and scenarios are provided at: http://www.careeronestop.org/competencym odel/pyramid.aspx?ENTRE=Y

6. After reviewing Activity 2 with the class, ask students: Why might being able to define and recognize competencies in yourself and others be important to the entrepreneur?

Answers will vary, but students should understand that recognizing competencies in yourself allows you to identify gaps in your education or experience. If you've identified gaps, you can fill them by taking courses, pursuing particular professional opportunities, or working towards particular licensures or certifications. Students should also understand that recognizing competencies in others is important when hiring employees and delegating work within a business. As an entrepreneur, you want to make sure that you're giving the right jobs in your business to the right people.

7. Explain to students that they will now analyze their own strengths and weaknesses as budding entrepreneurs. Hand out Activity 3: How Do I Know What I Need to Work On? Students should complete this activity individually.

8. Explain to students that nobody is good at everything, but that entrepreneurs see weaknesses as opportunities for improvement. There are a variety of ways that entrepreneurs can develop their human capital while "on the job." For example, the entrepreneur might seek out a mentor, a business leader who has "been there and done that" and who can offer the entrepreneur advice on his or her business and career. Networking through professional organizations and trade associations also allows the entrepreneur to connect with and learn from experts in their industry. However, hands-on experience plays a significant and critical part of the entrepreneurial growth continuum.

Successful entrepreneurs must be able to learn from their mistakes and apply the lessons they've learned to future decision-making.

9. Hand out Activity 4: What Next? Instruct students to use their self-assessment from Activity 3 to develop a plan of action for the future. Collect these action plans and provide students with personalized feedback, which might include recommendations for job and skills-training resources in the community.

CLOSURE

Summarize this lesson by discussing the following with the students:

1. What is human capital? Why is human capital important to the entrepreneur?

   Human capital is the education, experience, training, skills, and values of people. Human capital is important to the entrepreneur because, as a business leader, he or she must possess the education, experience, training, skills, and values to run their business successfully and ethically.

2. What is the relationship between education and human capital?

   Education is an investment in human capital. By educating yourself—whether through formal study at an institution or self-study—you increase your human capital by developing knowledge and acquiring skills.

3. What are ways in which you can develop your human capital?

   Human capital can be developed through formal study at a college or university, self-study, business-sponsored training programs, professional certification or licensure, on-the-job experiences, networking, and mentoring.

ASSESSMENT

Multiple-choice questions

1. Which of the following is an example of human capital?

   a. Money
   b. Opportunity cost
   c. *Analytical thinking**
   d. A factory

2. All of the following are ways to invest in human capital except:

   a. Receiving a college degree
   b. *Buying a car**
   c. On-the-job training
   d. Mentoring

Constructed-response questions

1. What is a competency model? How can using a competency model help you develop your human capital?

   A competency model provides a useful framework for thinking about the knowledge, skills, and abilities people need in order to perform successfully in a particular work setting. By comparing your current knowledge and skills against a competency model for a chosen occupation or industry, you can figure out what you need to work on in order to become successful in your career.

2. What are some examples of human capital you possess?

   Answers will vary, but possible responses include: abilities to read, write, compute, work in groups, play a sport, play an instrument, etc.

ACTIVITY 1
EDUCATION AND HUMAN CAPITAL

Education pays:

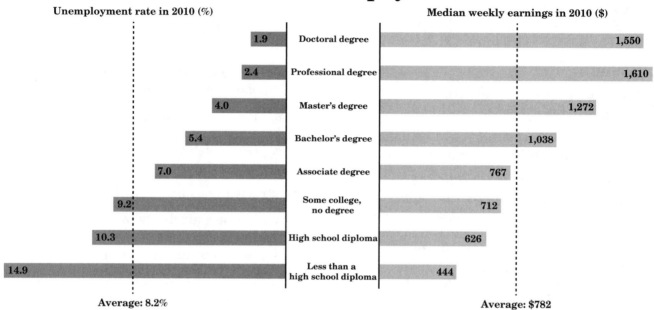

Unemployment rate in 2010 (%)   Median weekly earnings in 2010 ($)

	Unemployment rate in 2010 (%)	Education level	Median weekly earnings in 2010 ($)
	1.9	Doctoral degree	1,550
	2.4	Professional degree	1,610
	4.0	Master's degree	1,272
	5.4	Bachelor's degree	1,038
	7.0	Associate degree	767
	9.2	Some college, no degree	712
	10.3	High school diploma	626
	14.9	Less than a high school diploma	444

Average: 8.2%   Average: $782

Note: Data are 2010 annual averages for persons age 25 and over. Earnings are for full-time wage and salary workers.

Source: Bureau of Labor Statistics, Current Population Survey, http://www.bls.gov/emp/ep_chart_001.htm

a. What is the relationship between median weekly earnings and education level?

b. What is the relationship between unemployment rates and education levels?

c. What does this tell you about the impact of education on an individual's human capital and future economic opportunity?

d. Getting an education costs money. Based on your answers to the questions above, why might you be willing to spend money on educational opportunities?

ACTIVITY 2
ENTREPRENEURSHIP COMPETENCIES

Directions: Work with your group to create a definition for each of the competencies listed below. Using the definitions your group develops, list 1-2 specific ways you might assess whether or not an individual possesses a certain competency.

Personal Effectiveness Competencies		
Competency	What does this mean?	How does a person show this?
Interpersonal Skills		
Initiative		
Ambition		
Adaptability and Flexibility		
Willingness To Learn		
Willingness To Take Risks		

ACTIVITY 2, CONTINUED
ENTREPRENEURSHIP COMPETENCIES

Directions: Work with your group to create a definition for each of the competencies listed below. Using the definitions your group develops, list 1-2 specific ways you might assess whether or not an individual possesses a certain competency.

Academic Competencies		
Competency	What does this mean?	How does a person show this?
Reading		
Writing		
Mathematics		
Science & Technology		
Communication: Listening & Speaking		
Critical & Analytical Thinking		

ACTIVITY 2, CONTINUED
ENTREPRENEURSHIP COMPETENCIES

Directions: Work with your group to create a definition for each of the competencies listed below. Using the definitions your group develops, list 1-2 specific ways you might assess whether or not an individual possesses a certain competency.

Workplace Competencies		
Competency	What does this mean?	How does a person show this?
Creative Thinking		
Networking		
Planning & Organizing		
Checking, Examining & Recording		
Business Fundamentals		
Computer Applications		

ACTIVITY 3
HOW DO I KNOW WHAT I NEED TO WORK ON?

Directions : Assign a value 1 through 10 for each of the competencies, rating yourself and what you believe others think of you. 1 is lowest ("I do not demonstrate this" or "Others say I don't demonstrate this") and 10 is highest ("I demonstrate this all the time" or "Others say I demonstrate this all the time"). Add the two scores for each competency and write your total in the "Total Score" column.

	I think I demonstrate this	Others would say I demonstrate this	Total Score
Personal Effectiveness			
Interpersonal Skills			
Initiative			
Ambition			
Adaptability & Flexibility			
Willingness To Take Risks			
Willingness To Learn			
Academic Competencies			
Reading			
Writing			
Mathematics			
Science & Technology			
Communication:			
Listening & Speaking			
Critical & Analytical Thinking			
Workplace Competencies			
Creative Thinking			
Networking			
Planning & Organizing			
Problem Solving & Decision Making			
Checking, Examining, & Recording			
Business Fundamentals			
Computer Applications			

Activity 3, Continued
How Do I Know What I Need to Work On?

Look at your top scores. Which ones are the highest? Write them in order, highest to lowest:

1. _____

2. _____

3. _____

Look at your bottom scores. Which ones are the lowest? Write them in order, lowest to highest:

1. _____

2. _____

3. _____

ACTIVITY 4
WHAT NEXT?

Directions: Create an action plan for improving the areas of weakness you identified in Activity 3.

Competency To Be Worked On	Check as many as apply:					Actions To Be Taken
	Networking	Mentoring	Formal Education	On-the-Job	Self Train	
1.						1. 2. 3.
2.						1. 2. 3.
3.						1. 2. 3.

VISUAL 1
COMPETENCY MODELS AND HUMAN CAPITAL

Competency Model Building Blocks

Entrepreneurship Competency Model

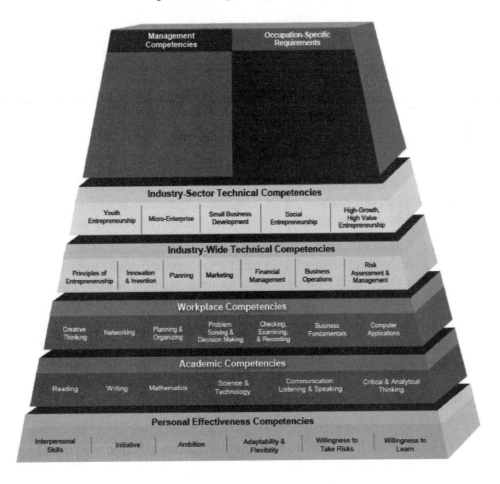

Source: CareerOneStop, U.S. Department of Labor, http://www.careeronestop.org/competencymodel/pyramind.aspx?ENTRE=Y

LESSON 10

TARGETING
THE MARKET

LESSON 10
TARGETING THE MARKET

LESSON DESCRIPTION

This lesson introduces students to **marketing** and its importance to the entrepreneur. Through a series of teacher-guided questions, students will think like entrepreneurs and "step into the consumer's shoes" in order to identify how a **product** can be marketed to satisfy diverse consumer wants. Students will place this thought exercise in the context of the marketing mix and target marketing. Through a hands-on matching activity, students will learn how the Four P's coalesce around a **target market**. They will then apply this knowledge to the lesson's culminating activity: the development of a successful marketing strategy for a given product.

INTRODUCTION

In order to gain a foothold against larger companies, entrepreneurs must know how to create, communicate, promote, and deliver goods and services of value to customers. They must also know how to identify who their customers are and what their customers want. Marketing encompasses all of the activities the entrepreneur undertakes to deliver and sell his or her product to potential customers.

CONCEPTS

- Marketing
- Product
- Target market
- Normal good
- Inferior good
- Substitute good
- Complementary good

OBJECTIVES

Students will:

1. Define and describe the 4 P's in the marketing mix.

2. Differentiate between **complementary good** and **substitute good**, **normal good** and **inferior good**.

3. Develop a marketing strategy for a given product by identifying a target market and creating a marketing mix.

TIME REQUIRED

Two class periods

MATERIALS

Activity 1: Which Type of Good?

Activity 2: Putting The Four P's Together

Activity 3: Define Your Target Market

Activity 4: Product Marketing Strategy

Visual 1: The Marketing Mix

Visual 2: Types of Goods

Visual 3: Market Segmentation Characteristics

PROCEDURE

1. Open the lesson by asking students the following question: What would you look for when buying a car?

   Answers will vary, but high school students will likely focus their discussion on the vehicle's physical appearance, such as model (convertible, sedan, or SUV), brand, and color.

2. Then ask students the following questions, one at a time: What might your parents look for when buying a car? What might a wealthy businessman look for when buying a car? What might a college student on a budget look for when buying a car?

ENTREPRENEURSHIP ECONOMICS © COUNCIL FOR ECONOMIC EDUCATION, NEW YORK, NY

Answers will vary, but encourage students to think about what each of these customers might focus on when buying a vehicle. Parents might focus on: safety features to keep their children and families out of harm's way; larger vehicle models, such as a van, station wagon, or SUV, that accommodate multiple passengers for carpooling to team practice, taking family vacations, etc.; price point and maintenance costs that are affordable and in keeping with the family budget. A wealthy businessman might focus on: a more expensive car with a recognizable brand that speaks to the businessman's success; luxury features that will impress clients, such as leather seats, sun-roof, and deluxe entertainment options; tinted windows for confidentiality and privacy. A college student on a budget might focus on: second-hand or used cars that offer affordability in purchase price, insurance costs, and maintenance costs.

3. Point out to students that, when they discussed the features they look for in a car, they were thinking about themselves, their preferences, and their interests. In other words, they were thinking like a consumer, or the person buying the product. When they discussed the features other people might want in a car, they began thinking like entrepreneurs, or the person selling the product. They were mentally producing a car that would satisfy the needs of individuals with different priorities, preferences, and tastes. Explain to students that business marketing revolves around identifying and satisfying consumer wants. By "standing in the consumer's shoes," the entrepreneur can recognize ways to sell their existing products and create new products that satisfy consumer wants.

4. Display Visual 1: The Marketing Mix, and tell students that the marketing mix—also known as The Four P's—provides entrepreneurs with a framework for thinking strategically about ways to market a product in order to satisfy a specific consumer audience, or target

market. Review the definitions provided in Visual 1 as a class. Reinforce student understanding of Visual 1 with the following explanation: As an entrepreneur, you need to develop a product with characteristics that will satisfy your target market's wants. You need to determine the price your target market is willing to pay for your product. You need to find out the places your target market would go to find and buy your product. And, finally, you need to promote your product in a way that ensures that your target market knows about it.

5. When students are comfortable with the concept of the marketing mix, remind students that entrepreneurs develop products around the Four P's to satisfy consumer wants. However, consumer wants are often influenced by outside economic factors, which can increase or decrease demand for a product. Economists therefore classify products as either complementary or substitute goods, normal or inferior goods. Display Visual 2: Types of Goods, and review the definitions provided with students. To reinforce student understanding of these concepts, hand out one copy of Activity 1: Which Type of Good? to each student. Once students have completed the activity, discuss their answers to the questions as a class.

Complementary vs. Substitute: Right and left shoes (C); Sweaters and sweatshirts (S); Hot dogs and ketchup (C); Nickels and dimes (S); Ice cream and sorbet (S); Pencils and markers (S); Gasoline and car (C); Flat screen TV and DVD player (C)

Normal vs. Inferior: Instant coffee (I); Public transportation (I); Hamburger (I); Sports convertible (N); Filet mignon steak (N); Frozen dinner (I); Designer jeans (N); New laptop computer (N)

6. Cut out the cards provided in Activity 2: Putting The Four P's Together, and place the cards into a paper bag at the front of the classroom. (Note that Activity 2 is designed to place students into seven

groups of four. There are 28 cards that create 7 distinct marketing mixes. Depending on the size of your class, you may need to adjust the number of card sets distributed.) Explain to students that their knowledge of the marketing mix and different types of goods will allow them to put together the Four P's for different products. Tell students that they will participate in a matching activity to demonstrate how the Four P's must logically fit together. Randomly call each student to the front of the class to pick one card from the bag until all cards have been chosen. Explain to students that each card belongs to one of the Four P's—and that their goal is to find the students in the class with the remaining P cards needed to complete their marketing mix. Instruct students to walk around the room asking one another about the contents of their cards to determine whether or not they relate to the same marketing mix. When they find a classmate with a P card that logically links with their own, they should team up with that classmate to find the remaining cards. By the end of activity, students should be standing in groups of four. While there is some potential for variation, the suggested groupings for the Four P card sets are:

Bottled Beverage—Vending Machine— $1.50—"Hydrate to the max."

Sweater—High-end retail store—$500— "Enjoy the expensive feel of soft cashmere."

Sneakers—Sports goods store—$75— "Hoop's the limit."

Camera—Electronics store—$120— "Excellent point-and-shoot value."

Jeans—Discount store—$35—"Casual fit for casual guys."

Car—Local dealership—$35,895—"Quality wheels built for your budget."

Frozen TV Dinner—Supermarket—$6.25— "Fast food that keeps you fit."

7. Tell students to work in their groups to

address the following: (1) Explain the group's reasoning about why the Four P's in the set should go together; (2) Identify whether or not the good is inferior or normal; and (3) Describe the target market the group thinks the product would appeal to, based on the Four P's. After students have developed answers, ask a student from each group to read aloud the Four P's in the group's card set and present the group's answers. Use these presentations as an opportunity to make any corrections using the following answers and explanations:

Four P Card Set Answers and Explanations:

Bottled beverage

(1) Answers will vary

(2) Inferior

(3) Answers will vary, but the promotional slogan emphasizes hydration, so the target market might be athletes or those who enjoy athletics. The use of "to the max" seems slightly slangy, so the target market may well be teenagers and young adults.

Sweater

(1) Answers will vary

(2) Normal

(3) Answers will vary, but the promotional slogan and price point indicate that the target market is most likely wealthy (or aspiring to be wealthy) and willing to spend a lot of money on clothing.

Sneakers

(1) Answers will vary

(2) Normal

(3) Answers will vary, but the promotional slogan and placement suggest that the target market is athletes, specifically basketball players.

Camera

(1) Answers will vary

(2) Normal

(3) Answers will vary, but the promotional slogan and comparative price point indicate that the camera is an affordable product targeted toward a budget-conscious target market.

Jeans

(1) Answers will vary

(2) Inferior

(3) Answers will vary, but the price point, placement, and promotional slogan all indicate that these jeans are for men unwilling to pay a higher price point for basic clothing items.

Car

(1) Answers will vary

(2) Normal

(3) Answers will vary, but the price point and promotional slogan indicate that this car would appeal to price-conscious buyers who are interested the long-term maintenance of the vehicle.

Frozen TV Dinner

(1) Answers will vary

(2) Inferior

(3) Answers will vary, but the target market is likely health-conscious shoppers on a budget.

8. After the Four P mini-presentations, instruct students to sit in their groups, and ask a student from each group to return the Price, Placement, and Promotion cards to the paper bags. Groups should keep their Product card. Ask students to imagine that they are entrepreneurs. They have a product idea, but they need to develop a marketing strategy in order to sell their product successfully. In order to develop the marketing strategy for their product, each group will take a two-step approach: (1) identify the target market for the product and (2) create a marketing mix for the product.

9. Display Visual 3: Market Segmentation Characteristics, and explain to students that effective entrepreneurs know how to think specifically about their target market in order to "stand inside the consumer's shoes." Explain that target markets can be broken down—or segmented—based on the following characteristics: Geographic, Demographic, Psychographic, and Behavioral. Review the characteristics associated with each category, and discuss how each of these characteristics might affect a product's marketing mix. To help students understand the difference between target markets and market segments, return to the example of the car provided at the beginning of the lesson. If your product is a car, you might choose women as your target market. However, a 22-year-old woman and a 50-year-old woman have different preferences and priorities when buying cars, so they represent two different segments of the target market. A 22-year-old woman might shop for different cars, at different prices, and in different places than a 50-year-old, so the promotion of the product might also be very different.

10. Hand out a copy of Activity 3: Define Your Target Market to each group, and instruct groups to work together to think about the market segment to whom they would like to sell their product. Remind students that there are no constraints on which segment they choose beyond thinking creatively.

11. Once students have completed Activity 3 and identified their target market as a group, hand out a copy of Activity 4: Product Marketing Strategy to each student. Instruct groups to begin the activity together by writing 3-4 sentences summarizing the characteristics of their target market, drawing on the information identified in Activity 4. Students should then assign each member of the group one of the Four P's and work individually to answer the relevant questions. Instruct students to record their answers to the questions in paragraph-form on a separate

sheet of paper, and encourage students to answer questions as specifically as possible. (For example, when thinking about the placement of their product, a group shouldn't just say "Supermarket." Students should push themselves to think about the following questions: What kind of supermarket? All supermarkets? Or a specific brand of supermarket? What aisle of the supermarket?) After each student in the group has completed the questions on the assigned P, groups should share their findings and discuss whether or not their Four P's fit together as a coherent marketing mix. Encourage students to revise and strengthen their marketing mix through this group discussion.

12. After groups have refined their marketing mix, tell students that they will deliver their product's marketing strategy in a presentation to the class, which will judge the strategy's success. Group presentations will need to answer the following questions: (1) Whom did the group choose as the target market for this product? Why? (2) What is the marketing mix for this product? How did the group create this marketing mix? Tell students that all four students in the group must participate in the presentation and that groups must decide how to structure their presentations effectively. (Depending on teacher preference, groups can prepare for their presentations in class or as a homework assignment.) After each presentation, the class should discuss whether or not the group's marketing strategy will be successful with their target market. Encourage students to identify what they believed to be the most and least effective elements of each group's marketing strategy and explain their reasoning within the context of the group's target market.

CLOSURE

Summarize the lesson by discussing the following questions with students:

1. What is a target market? Why is the

target market essential to developing a marketing strategy?

A target market is a group of consumers to whom a business wants to sell its products. Target marketing makes the promotion, pricing and placement of your products and/or services easier and more cost-effective. Target marketing provides a focus for all marketing activities. In order to develop its marketing strategy, a business must first identify its target market—and then build a marketing mix of Product, Placement, Price, and Promotion around that target market. Without a target market, the business does not have a focal point for its marketing activities.

2. What are the Four P's?

Product, Placement, Price, and Promotion

3. Why are the concepts of target market and the marketing mix crucial to entrepreneurial success?

In order to develop a marketing strategy for a given product, the entrepreneur must engage in a two-step process: (1) identify the target market for the product and (2) create a marketing mix for the product based on the target market's consumer wants.

ASSESSMENT

Multiple-choice questions

1. To develop a marketing strategy, the entrepreneur must:

   a. Develop a product and promote it to the consumer.
   b. *Identify a target market and develop a marketing mix.**
   c. Conduct marketing research and plan production.
   d. Price a product and distribute it to the customer.

2. Hotdogs and hotdog buns are examples of:

   a. Inferior and substitute goods
   b. Normal and inferior goods
   c. *Complementary goods**

d. Substitute goods

3. The 4 P's in a marketing mix include:

    a. People, Places, Products, Perishable
        goods
    b. Physical goods, Plastic goods, Plain
        goods, Paper goods
    c. Electronic Media, Print Media, Bulletin
        Boards, Advertisements
    d. *Product, Price, Placement, Promotion**

5. Brand Loyalty is a characteristic of which
    market segmentation?

    a. *Behavioristic**
    b. Demographic
    c. Geographic
    d. Psychographic

ACTIVITY 1
WHICH TYPE OF GOOD?

Complementary or Substitute?

Directions: For each good, write "C" for complementary or "S" for substitute.

Right and left shoes . . . . ._____

Sweaters and sweatshirts . . . . ._____

Hot dogs and ketchup . . . . ._____

Nickels and dimes . . . . ._____

Ice cream and sorbet . . . . ._____

Pencils and markers . . . . ._____

Gasoline and car . . . . ._____

Flat screen TV and DVD player . . . . ._____

Normal or Inferior?

Directions: For each good, write "N" for normal or "I" for inferior.

Instant coffee . . . . ._____

Public transportation . . . . ._____

Hamburger . . . . ._____

Sports convertible . . . . ._____

Filet mignon steak . . . . ._____

Frozen dinner . . . . ._____

Designer jeans . . . . ._____

New laptop computer . . . . ._____

ACTIVITY 2
PUTTING THE FOUR P'S TOGETHER

Directions: Cut out the following cards. Please note that these cards have been designed for a class of 28 students. Depending on the size of your class, you may need to adjust the number of card sets distributed.

Product: Bottled beverage	Placement: Vending machine	Price: $1.50	Promotional Slogan: "Hydrate to the max."
Product: Sweater	Placement: High-end retail store	Price: $500	Promotional Slogan: "Enjoy the expensive feel of soft cashmere."
Product: Sneakers	Placement: Sports goods store	Price: $75	Promotional Slogan: "Hoop's The Limit."
Product: Camera	Placement: Electronics store	Price: $120	Promotional Slogan: "Excellent point-and shoot value."
Product: Jeans	Placement: Discount store	Price: $35	Promotional Slogan: "Casual fit for casual guys."
Product: Car	Placement: Local dealership	Price: $35,895	Promotional Slogan: "Quality wheels built for your budget."
Product: Frozen TV Dinner	Placement: Supermarket	Price: $6.25	Promotional slogan: "Fast food that keeps you fit."

ACTIVITY 3
DEFINE YOUR TARGET MARKET

Directions: Define your target market by considering its geographic, demographic, psychographic, and behavioral characteristics. Circle all information that applies to your target market. The more specific you get, the better your marketing strategy will be.

GEOGRAPHIC

Describe the region(s) where your target market lives:

_____

_____

Population Density:

❑ Urban ❑ Suburban ❑ Rural

DEMOGRAPHIC

Age: ❑ 12-24	❑ 25-35	❑ 35-45	❑ 45-55	❑ 55-65	❑ 65-75	❑ 75 or older
Gender:	❑ Male	❑ Female	❑ Both			
Marital Status:	❑ Single	❑ Married	❑ Divorced	❑ Widowed		
Employment:	❑ Employed	❑ Unemployed	❑ Student	❑ Homemaker		
Size of Household: ❑ 1-5	❑ 5-10	❑ 10 or more				
# Children in Household: ❑ 0	❑ 1	❑ 2	❑ 3	❑ 4	❑ 5	❑ 6 or more
Highest Level of Education: ❑ High School	❑ College	❑ Graduate School				
Income Level: ❑ $0-$25K	❑ $25K-$50K	❑ $50K-$75K	❑ $75K-$100K	❑ Over $100K		

PSYCHOGRAPHIC

What are the hobbies and interests of your target market?

_____

_____

What is your target market's lifestyle? (Ex: Conservative, liberal, trendy, etc.)

_____

_____

ACTIVITY 3
DEFINE YOUR TARGET MARKET

What are characteristics your target market aspires to be? (Ex: Wealthy, cool, athletic, etc.)

_____

_____

What other items might your target market own? (Ex: A car, a pet, etc.)

_____

_____

BEHAVIORISTIC
How loyal is your target market to certain brands?

_____

_____

How often does your target market buy new things? What time of year does your target market typically buy things?

_____

_____

What special occasions does your target market celebrate?

_____

_____

What are some examples of other products your target market buys?

_____

_____

ACTIVITY 4
PRODUCT MARKETING STRATEGY

TARGET MARKET

Write a 3-4 sentence summary of the characteristics of your group's target market:

PRODUCT

1. What does the target market want from your product?

2. How will your product satisfy these wants? What will be the features of your product?

3. What will your product look like? How will your product be packaged?

4. What is your product's name/brand?

PRICE

1. How will you price your product?

2. How will your product's price compare to that of similar products?

3. How sensitive is your target market to price?

4. How will your product's price appeal to your target market?

PLACEMENT

1. Where does your target market typically shop for products that are similar to yours?

2. Are there any other locations where your target market would shop for your product?

3. Where will you sell your product? (Include relevant store names, locations within the store, geographical locations, etc.)

4. Can you sell your product in-stores or online? Or both?

PROMOTION

1. How does your target market typically learn about products similar to yours?

2. How will you let your target market know about your product?

3. When is the best time to promote your product? Are there specific times of year when your target market buys your product or spends more?

4. How do your competitors promote their similar products? What can you learn from them?

VISUAL 1
THE MARKETING MIX

TARGET MARKET

A target market is a group of consumers to whom a business wants to sell its products.

Examples: women, men, parents, teenagers, college students, athletes, pet owners, etc.

PRODUCT

The good or service offered to satisfy a customer's want.

PRICE

Establishing and communicating the value of a good or a service to the prospective customer.

THE MARKETING MIX "THE FOUR P'S"

PLACEMENT

Any form of communication used to inform, persuade, or remind consumers about the product.

PROMOTION

The channel or pathway used to get both the marketing message and the product to the consumer. The channel could be direct from producer to the final consumer of via the use of a supply chain (intermediaries such as wholesalers, distributors, and retailers).

VISUAL 2
TYPES OF GOODS

COMPLEMENTARY GOODS

Goods that go together or complement one another; i.e. hot dogs and hot dog buns, cake and ice cream, shoes and shoe laces.

VS.

SUBSTITUTE GOODS

Goods that have a similar function; however, if the price of one good starts to up, then people will substitute another good in its place.

NORMAL GOODS

Those goods for which consumers' demand increases when their income increases.

VS.

INFERIOR GOODS

Goods that decrease in demand when consumer income rises. These goods are not of poorer quality than other goods, as is suggested by the adjective "inferior." Instead, they are simply goods that you consume less of if your income rises.

VISUAL 3

MARKET SEGMENTATION CHARACTERISTICS

GEOGRAPHIC:

- Region (Country, State, Neighborhood, City)
- Population Density (Urban, Suburban, Rural)
- Climate (Weather patterns)

DEMOGRAPHIC:

- Age
- Gender
- Family Size
- Income
- Occupation
- Education
- Nationality
- Ethnicity
- Social Class

PSYCHOGRAPHIC:

- Hobbies/Interests
- Opinions
- Attitudes
- Values

BEHAVIORISTIC:

- Brand Loyalty
- Ability and Willingness to Buy
- Occasion (Valentine's Day, Christmas, Birthday, Wedding, Anniversary, etc.)

LESSON 11
THE BUSINESS PLAN

LESSON DESCRIPTION

In this lesson, students will explore the importance of **opportunity recognition**, business planning, and business presentation. Students will conduct an informal gap analysis and analyze demographic data in order to identify business opportunities in their community. Students will then work in small groups to develop new business ideas based on the opportunities they've recognized. After learning about the components of a successful business plan, students will construct detailed plans for their new businesses. Finally, students will create a 30-second elevator pitch that communicates their business idea and plan to the class.

INTRODUCTION

If a person wants to travel from point A to point B, he or she needs to have an idea of how to get there—or at least a good map. Starting a business is no different. In order to build a viable business, the entrepreneur must know what the business's goals are and how to achieve those goals. The **business plan** provides entrepreneurs with a framework for thinking about what they will need to develop and maintain a profitable business. Indeed, the business plan requires entrepreneurs to consider every aspect of their business's vision, management, and financial plan as well as strategies for building their business and timelines for critical decision-making.

While the business plan is critical to the business internally, the business plan is also critical to securing start-up funding. Lenders—whether traditional lenders, such as banks and credit unions—or non-traditional lenders—such as microfinance programs or angel investors—immediately look to a business plan when considering lending options. These institutions see the business plan as an immediate overview of the company's present health and a predictor of the company's future potential. Lenders are reluctant to loan to companies that do not have

a well-developed business plan, as they are unsure that the entrepreneur has spent the time and effort to think deeply about how to make his or her business financially profitable.

There are many companies and websites that claim that they can write a business plan guaranteed to receive funding. However, unless the entrepreneur is directly involved in creating the business plan, the document may not reflect the business's current vision or its potential for future success. By the same token, the entrepreneur should consider the business plan a living document that accommodates changes to the business over time and requires ongoing planning, development, implementation, and evaluation.

CONCEPTS

- Opportunity recognition
- Business plan

OBJECTIVES

Students will:

1. Conduct a gap analysis in order to identify potential business opportunities in their local community

2. Analyze demographic data in order to identify potential business opportunities

3. Describe the purpose of the business plan and understand the impact of an effective business plan on business financing and long-term business success

4. Create business plans and develop strategies for concisely communicating their business ideas

TIME REQUIRED

Three class periods

MATERIALS

Activity 1: Gap Analysis Chart

Activity 2: Demographic Data Analysis

Activity 3: From Data To Dollar Signs

Activity 4: Building the Plan

Activity 5: Presenting the Plan: The 30-Second Elevator Pitch

Visual 1: The Business Plan

Visual 2: Elevator Pitch Essentials

PROCEDURE

1. Explain to students that surveying and evaluating old business ideas can often lead entrepreneurs to new business ideas. Hand out Activity 1: Gap Analysis Chart. Ask students: What businesses already exist in our local community? Allow the class to brainstorm examples of different local businesses. Students should record their examples in the first column on the chart. After students are finished brainstorming, discuss their examples as a class.

Possible business examples: coffee shop, restaurant, dog grooming, lawn care, computer repair, babysitting, etc.

Prompt students to think about whether any of the local business examples are not as good as they could be. Ask students: How would you improve these businesses? Students should record their suggestions in the second column of the chart. Discuss students' suggestions as a class.

Possible suggestions for improvement: better service or additional service, more variety, more creativity, etc.

Finally, encourage students to think about local businesses that do not exist. Ask students: What businesses are "missing" from our community? Is there a business that you wish we had? Tell students not to be afraid of "outrageous" ideas. You might throw out a potentially "outrageous" idea to get students thinking. (You might say, "I am really sick of doing my laundry. I really wish there was a business in town that sold robots. Then they could do all of my laundry for me.") Students should record their new business ideas in the third column of the chart. Discuss students' business ideas as a class.

2. Reveal to students that surveying and evaluating the current business landscape is called conducting a gap analysis. Ask students: Why do you think conducting a gap analysis might be an important first step for entrepreneurs?

Possible answers include: you don't "re-invent the wheel" or duplicate another person's business idea; you figure out what people might want in a business that isn't currently being provided by other businesses and make money off of that knowledge.

3. Tell students that you can fill gaps with new business ideas. Explain that entrepreneurs can often recognize these gaps simply by surveying their surroundings. However, conducting research and analyzing data provide the entrepreneur with valuable information that can strengthen their business idea formation. For example, in the United States, age demographics are changing rapidly. These changing demographics can provide entrepreneurs with valuable information about existing and future opportunities. Place students into groups of four, and distribute Activity 2: Demographic Data Analysis. Point out that the two visuals paint an interesting picture of an aging population. Ask students to work in their groups to answer the questions. Discuss students' answers to the questions as a class.

a. What does the first graph represent?

Resident Population of the United States as of July 1, 1990

b. What does the second graph represent?

Projected Resident Population of the United States as of July 1, 2025

c. How would you describe the shape of the first graph?

Curvy, wide in the middle and narrowing toward the top

d. How would you describe the shape of the second graph?

Boxy, sides are relatively straight and become narrow at the very top

e. What is on the Y axis?

Age in five-year segments

f. What is on the X axis?

The percent of males and females in age ranges

g. How many age segments exceeded 7 percent of the population in 1990 – hint: add male and female percentages at each age segment?

8 segments – under 5, 5-9, 15-19, 20-24, 25-29, 30-34, 35-39, 40-44

h. How many age segments are projected to exceed 7 percent of the population in 2025?

0

i. In what 2025 age segment are the people who were 30 to 34 years old in 1990?

They are in the 65 to 69 age segment.

j. Approximately what percentage of the population consisted of 65- to 69-year olds in 1990?

4 percent

k. Approximately what percentage of the population will consist of 65- to 69-year olds in 2025?

Accept any answers from 5.75 percent to 6 percent.

l. How old is the 1990 30- to 34-year old segment today?

In 2012, the segment is 52 to 56; 2013: 53 to 57; 2014: 54 to 58; and so on.

m. What generalization can you draw from looking at the two graphs?

The population is aging; there are more females than males after middle age.

4. Explain that age is an important demographic for entrepreneurs to be aware of because people of different ages want different goods and services. Ask the following questions and record the answers on the board.

a. What goods and services are important to people who are 30-34 years old?

Answers will vary but could include babysitter services, piano lessons for their children, restaurants and nightclubs, personal communication devices, swimming pools, gyms.

b. What goods and services are important to people who are 55-59 years old?

Answers will vary but could include restaurants, gyms, hair stylists, personal communication devices, auto detailing.

c. What goods and services are important to people who are 65-69 years old?

Answers will vary but could include golf courses, restaurants, hair stylists, auto detailing, health services, travel services.

Tell students that each of these age segments represents potential customers for the entrepreneur, and this can be important for the students now and when they get older.

5. Divide the class into small groups of three to four students. (Note: These groups will continue to work with one another throughout the remainder of the lesson's activities.) Hand out Activity 3: From Data To Dollar Signs. Tell students that they will be working in groups to use their local gap analysis and demographic data analysis to develop ideas for a new business. Each group's immediate task is to figure out how to take the information they've gathered from the data analysis

and the gap analysis and turn it into a money-making business idea. You may ask groups to partner with one another for feedback after the activity has been completed.

6. Tell students that, now that they have a business idea, they may feel ready to jump right into their business. However, even though they've done some initial thinking about their business, it's important and valuable to sketch out more clearly as many aspects of the business as possible. Display Visual 1: The Business Plan or provide as a hand-out to students. Read aloud the definition of a business plan and discuss the reasons for creating a business plan as well as its main features. Explain to students that successful business plans are highly detailed documents that provide an overview of the company's present health and future potential.

7. Distribute Activity 4: Building the Plan. Instruct students to work in their groups to fill out the business plan worksheet as completely as possible. Explain that, in the interest of time, the class will focus on the condensed business plan that makes up this activity. Completing this plan may require students up to a full class period to complete and may be assigned as homework. Students may also be encouraged to split up parts of the business plan and work individually on different sections to complete this worksheet in a timely manner.

8. With their business plans complete, students should now begin to work on presenting their business ideas and plans. Explain that business plan presentation is important for securing funding and generating interest in the business. Tell students that they need to be ready to communicate their business plan on the spot because they never know when the opportunity to fund their business might strike.

Ask students to imagine that they walk into an elevator and find the world's richest man inside. Tell students that they will have the duration of the elevator ride (30 seconds) to get the world's richest man to fund their business idea.

In order to get students excited about giving the presentations, show filmed clips of elevator pitches, which can be found at the following sites:
http://www.youtube.com/watch?v=vAvErchnM_w
http://www.youtube.com/watch?v=8SPVtJKMDOo

9. Display Visual 2: Elevator Pitch Essentials. Tell students that while there is not one "right" way to present a business plan in an elevator pitch, it is important that they get to the "meat of the matter" fairly quickly. To do this, students will need to make sure that they hit the "key points." Review Visual 2 with students, making sure that they understand the "Four P's" and other essential questions that will be useful to them in planning their 30-second pitch.

10. Distribute Activity 3: Presenting The Plan: The 30-Second Elevator Pitch. Instruct students to decide who will serve as their business's "speaker" to deliver the 30-second pitch to the class. Student groups should be given time to plan and rehearse before delivering their pitch to the class.

Depending on access to technology, you may choose to film the presentations for later review. You may also choose to invite outside experts, such as business owners, bankers, or industry professionals, to serve as reviewers.

CLOSURE

Summarize this lesson by discussing the following questions with students:

1. Why is the business plan important to entrepreneurs?

   The business plan provides a framework for the entrepreneur to develop his or her business idea and provides a document for potential lenders to refer to when considering whether or not to finance the business.

2. What information should be included in the business plan?

The business's name, its goals and objectives, the product(s) sold and distributed, the work skills needed to produce those products, and the marketing strategies used to promote them.

3. Why should you be able to communicate your business idea succinctly?

You never know when you will have the opportunity to transform your business plan into business reality.

potential markets that are growing and shrinking.

2. Why is it important for a potential funder to understand your business plan?

They will want to understand whether or not your business is viable before the decide to give you money; if you don't have a business plan, the potential funder will not think that you have put in the necessary time and effort to increase the odds of your business being successful.

ASSESSMENT

Multiple-choice questions

1. Which of the following describes the process of identifying potential business opportunities by surveying and assessing existing businesses?

   a. Promotion
   b. Business plan
   c. *Gap analysis**
   d. Market research

2. What are the Four P's?

   a. Product, price, population, program
   b. *Product, price, place, promotion**
   c. Place, program, price, presentation
   d. Promotion, price, presentation, program

3. Which of the following belong in a business plan?

   a. Marketing research
   b. Financing plan
   c. Management structure
   d. *All of the above**

Constructed-response questions

1. How can demographic data help you to identify an entrepreneurial opportunity?

People of different ages want different goods and services; by identifying the number of people who will fall within a certain age segment in future years you can recognize

ACTIVITY 1
GAP ANALYSIS CHART

Already Exist?	Could Be Improved?	Missing?

ACTIVITY 2

DEMOGRAPHIC DATA ANALYSIS

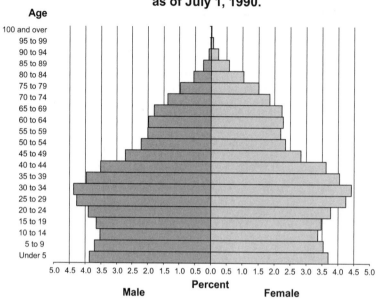

(NP-P1) Resident Population of the United States as of July 1, 1990.

Source: National Estimates Program, Population Division, U.S. Census Bureau, http://www.census.gov/population/www/projections/np_p1.pdf

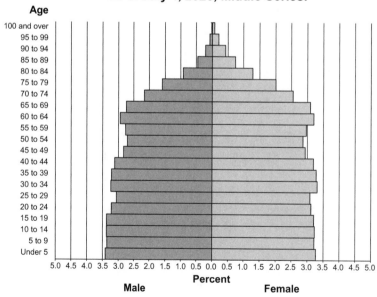

(NP-P3) Projected Resident Population of the United States as of July 1, 2025, Middle Series.

Source: National Estimates Program, Population Division, U.S. Census Bureau, http://www.census.gov/population/www/projections/np_p3.pdf

ACTIVITY 2, CONTINUED
DEMOGRAPHIC DATA ANALYSIS

Directions: Use the two populations graphs to answer the following questions.

a. What does the first graph represent?

b. What does the second graph represent?

c. How would you describe the shape of the first graph?

d. How would you describe the shape of the second graph?

e. What is on the Y axis?

f. What is on the X axis?

g. How many age segments exceeded 7 percent of the population in 1990 – hint: add male and female percentages at each age segment?

h. How many age segments are projected to exceed 7 percent of the population in 2025?

i. In what 2025 age segment are the people who were 30 to 34 years old in 1990?

j. Approximately what percentage of the population consisted of 65- to 69-year olds in 1990?

k. Approximately what percentage of the population will consist of 65- to 69-year olds in 2025?

l. How old is the 1990 30- to 34-year old segment today?

m. What generalization can you draw from looking at the two graphs?

ACTIVITY 3
FROM DATA TO DOLLAR SIGNS

Directions: The purpose of this activity is for your group to propose a business idea for development. Your first task as an entrepreneur is to communicate how your business will make money by answering the questions below.

1. Based on the information you've gathered about your local community and age demographics in the United States, what type of business would you choose to develop? Why?

2. What product and/or service will you sell?

3. What "gap" in the local community will your business fill?

4. Which age group provides the potential customers for your business? (You may choose more than one.)

5. Name some special features of your good or service that would attract the age group you are targeting.

6. How would you draw the attention of people in this age group to your business?

7. How much would you charge for this good or service?

8. Could this business be modified to make it a practical opportunity for you to begin now?

ACTIVITY 4
BUILDING THE PLAN

Directions: Discuss the following questions with your group and record your group's answers on a separate sheet of paper.

DESCRIPTION OF THE BUSINESS:

Name of firm:

Owners (Anyone with an investment in the firm):

Hours of Operation:

Location:

THE PRODUCT:

Describe your business, product, or service:

How is your product or service different from current products or services on the market?

When do you plan to start your business?

FOR COMPANIES SELLING PRODUCTS:

If creating a product, how do you make it?

How do you distribute your product to your customers? List outlets: (Retail, wholesale, phone or mail orders, telemarketing, Internet, personal selling, etc.)

FOR COMPANIES SELLING SERVICES:

How much time will it take you to perform your service? (Average per customer)

Are there others in your area selling the same service? (Who is your competition?)

What do they charge for their services?

How will you price your services or products?

THE MARKET:

What is the next big thing in your industry?

Who is your typical customer? For consumers discuss things such as age, sex, income, profession, lifestyle, education, family size, etc. For businesses discuss things such as type of business, sales, size, number of employees, number of years in business, etc.

Where are your customers located?

What is the size of your market? (How large of an area do you plan to sell to?)

What are your competitors' strengths and weaknesses?

What is your competitive advantage? How is your business different (or better) from your competitors?

ACTIVITY 4, CONTINUED
BUILDING THE PLAN

ADVERTISING AND MARKETING:

Who will sell your products or services? How? This includes meetings or phone calls by you, a sales force, or reps.

How will you promote or advertise your business?

What promotional marketing material will you develop (ads, catalogs, brochures, flyers, etc.)?

MANAGEMENT:

Identify the management and key personnel.

Name:

Title/Role:

FACILITIES:

Describe your business location including the building, physical features, age, dimensions, parking, etc.

Do you plan to lease or own the building?

Why did you choose this location?

What are the major items of equipment used in your business?

What other businesses are in the area that may have an effect on your business?

Are you close (in miles) to your customers?

FINANCIAL REQUIREMENTS:

Will you need external funding?

How much money will you need to start your business?

Will you consider borrowing?

Will you be using equity financing?

For how long do you want to borrow the money?

How much will the monthly payment be?

What do you intend to do with the money?

APPENDICES:

- Copies of business brochures (if any)
- Local map pinpointing business location

ACTIVITY 5
PRESENTING THE PLAN: THE 30-SECOND ELEVATOR PITCH

You walk into a crowded elevator, and somebody whispers in your ear, "Can you believe it? The richest man in the world is standing right next to you!" You immediately recognize this as an opportunity to get your group's business plan funded, but time is already running out. You have 30 seconds to convince the world's richest man that your business idea is an excellent one and that he should provide you with the funding you need to get your business up and running.

Your group will have exactly 30 seconds (and 30 seconds only!) to pitch your business idea to the world's richest man in front of the class, who will judge whether or not you succeeded in communicating your business idea in a compelling way.

Your group's task:

1. Decide who will be in the elevator! Who will serve as your business's "speaker"?

2. Make an outline that uses the Elevator Pitch Essentials to deliver your message about your business idea.

3. Make your speaker practice, practice, practice! Provide your speaker with feedback about what convinced you about their speech and what didn't.

VISUAL 1
THE BUSINESS PLAN

Business Plan: A description of an enterprise including its name, its goals and objectives, the product(s) sold and distributed, the work skills needed to produce those products, and the marketing strategies used to promote them.

Why create a business plan?

The business plan provides entrepreneurs with a framework for thinking about what they will need to develop and maintain a profitable business. Indeed, the business plan requires entrepreneurs to consider every aspect of their business's vision, management, and financial plan as well as strategies for building their business and timelines for critical decision-making. The effective entrepreneur considers the business plan as a living document that accommodates changes to the business over time and requires ongoing planning, development, implementation, and evaluation.

Who wants to see a business plan?

Lenders—whether traditional lenders, such as banks and credit unions, or non-traditional lenders, such as microfinance programs or angel investors, immediately look to a business plan when considering lending options. These institutions see the business plan as an immediate overview of the company's present health and a predictor of the company's profit potential. Lenders are reluctant to loan to companies that do not have a well developed business plan, as they are unsure that the entrepreneur has spent the time and effort to think deeply about how to make their business financially profitable.

What questions do business plans answer?

Business plans should:

- outline your business idea

- identify short- and long-term goals for your business

- describe why you think your business will succeed in a competitive marketplace and what research you have to back this up

- outline your plans to market your business

- describe how the business will be structured and managed

- include projected income statements and other financial data that demonstrates how the business will be financed and, eventually, profitable

VISUAL 2

ELEVATOR PITCH ESSENTIALS

The Four P's:

Product – What is the product(s) or service being sold?

Price – What is the price of the product(s) or service?

Placement – Where will the business operate? Where will the customers be located?

Promotion – What will be done to attract customers in a highly competitive environment?

Other questions you should consider...

Competitive advantage – Why will you succeed in a competitive business environment?

Market – Who are your customers and where are they located?

Funding requirements – How much (if any) money will you need and where will it come from?

Management – Who are the owners/managers of your company?